Walks in Wensleydale

by
Geoffrey White

Dalesman Books
1987

The Dalesman Publishing Company Ltd.,
Clapham, via Lancaster, LA2 8EB.

First published 1975
Fifth edition 1987

ISBN: 0 85206 883 2

To my wife at home
and daughter abroad
remembering especially
when we could see Penhill from home.

Printed by Fretwell & Cox Ltd., Goulbourne St., Keighley, West Yorkshire BD21 1PZ.

Contents

Front cover drawing of Gayle by Janet Rawlins.

The maps are by the author and the drawings in the text are by Geoffrey Green.

The author acknowledges with gratitude the assitance given by Norman Hancock and Geoffrey Green.

Foreword

MAN is a sentient being; happy then the man whose sentience gives his life the tone and colour of full enjoyment. Even happier is he who also — loving the open country — by grace or good fortune finds his habitat within the region of his beloved country dearest to him. Such a one is Geoffrey White, whose temperament is finely tuned not only to derive maximum personal satisfaction from walking in country ways but also to pass on to others by word and deed the intensity of that joy. His sentiments have much in common with Marlow's Passionate Shepherd who cried:

Come live with me and be my love,
And we will all the pleasures prove,
That hills and valleys, dales and fields,
Woods or steeply mountains, yield,

and right well he practises what he preaches.

Writing lovingly — as he must — of Wensleydale, the author finds himself, as do many others, quite unable to dissociate Swaledale from it. Nature must have been in a singularly playful mood when ordaining them as neighbours — widely differing yet linked physically and in human characteristics — for nowhere else in this England can one find two such geographically close yet dissimilar dales, the one all graciousness, restfulness and green charm, the other remote, detached, rugged and awesome but inexpressibly grand. He would be a brave man indeed who ventured upon a preference, and let him beware who voiced his choice to a native of the other.

Their rivers differ in like manner; for the Swale it is variously claimed to be the swiftest flowing in England, 'that wondrous holy flood,' and from its use by Paulinus in baptising, 'the Jordan of England'; but the Yore (for this Wensleydale is Yoredale) variously known as Ure, Yure, Eure, Jore, Jure, Jor and Yer, is the very waterland of York as its Aryan name-root proves — 'to the eye and ear all cool and clear' — with quiet and verdant banking lands, providing peaceful serenity soothing to man.

Historically they are as significant as industrially — indeed the two aspects tend to be inseparable — the Romans mining lead and coal whilst resident here as a base; the Scropes and Mary Queen of Scots being here by virtue of their very isolation; whilst the famous knitters of this dale combine both.

Semer Water

The author — as myself — has found and felt the mood and spirit of each, has loved and cherished the discovery, and has imaginatively reflected this in walks — themselves cleverly graded to suit all manner of walker — presented here for Wensleydale and in a separate book for Swaledale. If he has not wholly persuaded you, dear reader, of their worth, let you venture forth to what, I believe, must in the end be conversion and conviction.

Geoffrey Green

Introduction

ALTHOUGH the Yorkshire Dales National Park becomes more popular year by year with both motorist and walker, even the most enthusiastic Dales lover cannot be expected to have an intimate knowledge of all the nooks and crannies in it. This book attempts to fill some of the gaps, but by no means all, as well as effecting an introduction to the newcomer. All the walks are circular and they vary in length. To those finding them not long enough may I suggest combining two adjoining walks— with perhaps a short motor ride between? Long distance walkers could no doubt devise their own connecting links or find some value in the list of recognised long walks in the appendix. If a walk ever departs from the right of way it will be clearly stated. Only on the high fells will this occur, and here there is a tradition of public access — a privilege not a right. On open moors and fells I have never been denied the privilege, but on rare occasions when shooting parties have been encountered I have given the guns a wide berth!

The dale and its surroundings have everything to commend them: wild fell; outstanding views; extensive moorland; well-trodden tracks; places of historical and geographical interest; geological characteristics giving distinctive shapes to the hills and valleys; waterfalls of beauty and charm. Many books have been written about this delightful countryside, some being quoted in the appendix. I would commend *Yorkshire Dales National Park* published by Her Majesty's Stationery Office, a major purpose of which is to enable discerning visitors to understand the distinctiveness of the region, past and present, and, in seeing how the landscape has evolved, perhaps come to share some of the concern for it that is held by those who know it well. Another book of great authority is *The Yorkshire Dales,* an Aldine Paperback by Marie Hartley and Joan Ingilby, famous authors who have lived in Askrigg for a great number of years and are as familar with the Dales as any writer living. In reading their chapters on Wensleydsale, Coverdale, Bishopdale and Walden a considerable contribution is made to the interest of the fifteen walks covered by this book.

The map for each walk is intended to be self-explanatory, but the reader is recommended to use in addition the Ordnance Survey Map Sheet 98 (Wensleydale and Wharfedale, 1:50,000) for pleasure, interest and safety of the excursion. For Walks 1, 2, 3 and

4 the appropriate map is sheet 99 (Ripon). It may help the newcomer to make a start if I indicate my favourites among the walks at the time of writing:

	Short	Longer
Fell	Walk No. 8	12
Waterfalls	Walk No. 10	11
Places of interest	Walk No. 1	4

These are really good walks, not detracting in any way from others. In fact one wonders how much one is influenced by weather conditions on days of reconnaissance.

What to wear: Strong footwear — my own preference is for walking boots for the support they give to the ankles, grip on the ground and resistance to bog; thick socks — some prefer two pairs — even three; warm clothing.

What to carry: Waterproof — preferably anorak or cagoule; this guide; O.S. map; compass — chiefly for interest but you may get lost in mist; rucksack; some food, even if it is your intention to return for a meal; a simple first aid kit.

If the weather turns bad, do not hesitate to return by the way you have come. Conditions in the Dales can change very quickly, cloud or snow storms altering the outlook in minutes.

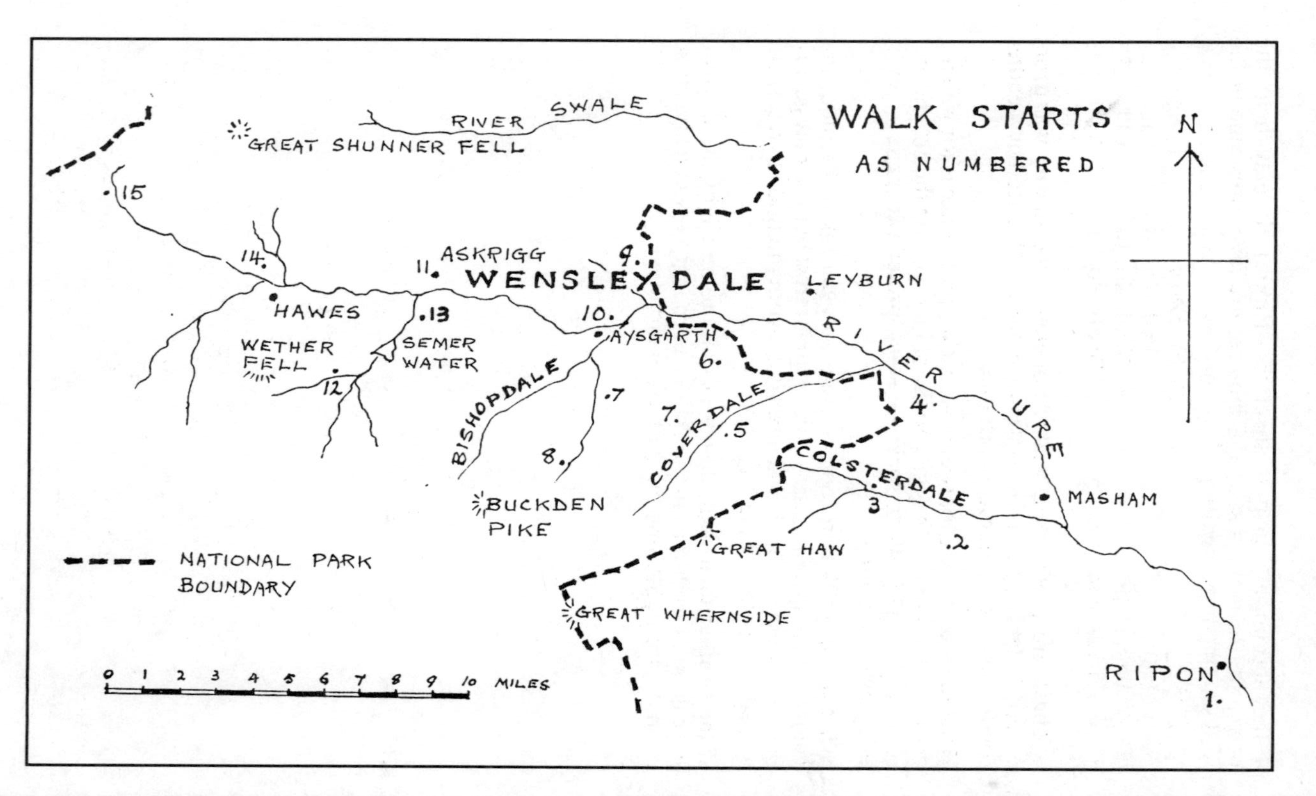
WALK STARTS
AS NUMBERED
N
RIVER SWALE
GREAT SHUNNER FELL
15
14.
11.
ASKRIGG
9.
WENSLEY DALE
LEYBURN
HAWES
.13
10.
AYSGARTH
RIVER URE
WETHER
FELL
SEMER
WATER
12
6.
BISHOPDALE
.7
7.
COVER DALE
.5
4.
8.
COLSTERDALE
3
MASHAM
BUCKDEN
PIKE
GREAT HAW
.2
NATIONAL PARK
BOUNDARY
GREAT WHERNSIDE
0 1 2 3 4 5 6 7 8 9 10 MILES
RIPON
1.

Wensleydale

FORMERLY called Yoredale or Uredale — the river gave it its name — the wide, green, wooded Wensleydale is distinctive for its size and beauty, famous for its cheese, and perhaps better known to road users than to pedestrians, although the five-pronged head of the dale has long been favourite walking country. Now that the Pennine Way passes through the dale, ramblers know it even better. The motorist's best broad picture of Wensleydale is probably from Scarth Nick on Preston Scar, above Redmire. Those arriving from the north-east will see Penhill across the valley, Bishopdale to its right, and then the head of the dale, lying to the right of the dinstinctive shape of the hill called Addlebrough. In between, the river Ure snakes through beautifully wooded country. Approaching from Masham, a good general view is obtained by walking up Witton Fell (see Walk 3). On the other side can be seen the terraced hills and scars of the Yoredale Series of limestones. This vantage point also gives a reminder of the place of Wensleydale in history. Below is Middleham Castle, associated with Richard III. Bolton Castle — ancestral home of the Scropes — is in the middle distance, and Jervaulx Abbey is away to the right.

The head of the dale is on the Cumbria and Noth Yorkshire border at Hell Gill. Almost certainly, the party bringing Mary Queen of Scots to her imprisonment in Bolton Castle would pass over Hell Gill Bridge and first see Wensleydale on the old High Way, now a green track. But it is the Pennine wayfarers, travelling northwards, whose first look at the dale from Ten End Fell, gives them the finest comprehensive view to the east, embracing the whole of this lovely region.

The foot of the dale is not so well defined as its head. In its turn Wensley Bridge has been suggested. Wensley, now a small village of exquisite charm, was once a market town, giving its name to the dale. Bolton Hall — the seat of Lord Bolton — is here, its wooded parkland contributing so much to the character of this part of the dale. Cover Bridge, beloved by fishermen, has also been proffered as the dale end. Still lower down the river, Kilgram Bridge may be taken as the boundary. But who can dispute it if the dwellers of Bedale and Masham claim to live in Wensleydale?

Waterfalls, caused by the differing resistance to weathering of limestone and shale, are a constant delight in the side valleys of this 'family of dales.' But the most famous of all are at Aysgarth. Also in the main valley is Hardraw Force, 99 feet high, England's highest fall above ground.

A big geological influence upon the shape of Wensleydale was the Ice Age. U-shaped valleys were gouged out by glaciers and in these flat valley bottoms lakes appeared when the meltwaters were dammed by moraines. Semer Water, one of Yorkshire's few natural lakes, is the only one remaining in the dale. Drumlins — well-moulded humps of rock debris and boulder clay — are conspicuous, especially in the area above Aysgarth.

My first experience of Wensleydale was on a schoolboy cycling tour, travelling down-dale from Widdale and Hawes. It was Whit Sunday; the slanting sun gave ethereal beauty to the fells and woodlands ahead of us; the calm evening, a slight following wind, and the downward slope gave us freewheeling pleasure. Ringing across the vale as we sped silently on the uncluttered road, church bells added the final touch of peace and tranquility. The memory of those moments has stayed with me for more than half a century. On today's busy roads it would be difficult to repeat the experience, but similar harmony can arise on foot in the hills and valleys — especially at the end of a day on the tops. It is my wish that such moments may fall to your lot.

Walk 1 **7½ or 6 miles**

Ripon and Fountains Abbey

RIPON, in a stretch of rolling open country, is not in Wensleydale, but from the south and south-west it is the gateway to it. Fountains Abbey is one of Britain's most famous national monuments and now in the care of the National Trust. For years it was the overlord of the dales and so beautifully situated in upland country, makes the perfect objective for the first walk of this volume. Ripon itself is a small attractive market town on the river Ure, with a cathedral going back to the fifteenth century — the west front is particularly fine. It is a city of tradition, notably in the blowing of the Wakeman's horn at nine o'clock every evening at the Mayor's house and at the market cross.

Those who prefer the shorter route will be able to pick it up from the car park through Studley Roger. The journey now to be described will be the whole of the longer route, the mileage being calculated from the bridge over the river Laver, just outside the city boundary on the Pateley Bridge road. Walking from the centre of Ripon adds a mile and a half to the longer walk.

Walking on the Pateley Bridge road, about 300 yards beyond the bridge (round the first bend), there is a signpost on the left indicating the footpath to Studley Roger. Go over the stile by the side of it and take a faint track through the centre of the field, towards the church spire seen ahead. Pass through a small gate in a post and rail fence; go over a substantial stile over an electric fence; make towards the left-hand corner of the field, in line with the village which is now in sight; pass two gnarled trees; and go through a gate into a short lane leading to the village street — delightful, quiet and clean.

Cross the road and follow a sign pointing the way to Fountains Abbey. Go over a churned-up field to a stile over a barbed wire fence; pass through a clean pasture to a gate in the wall of Studley Royal Park; and continue on the track through the park, where deer abound, to reach the straight park road at a point opposite an ice house. This is below a small copse on the opposite hillside. Turn to the right on the road and at the cross roads look back for a grand view of Ripon cathedral beyond the end of the drive. Now turn down to the lake, following the sign to the car park and Fountains Abbey. Still on the park road, keep alongside the delightful lake

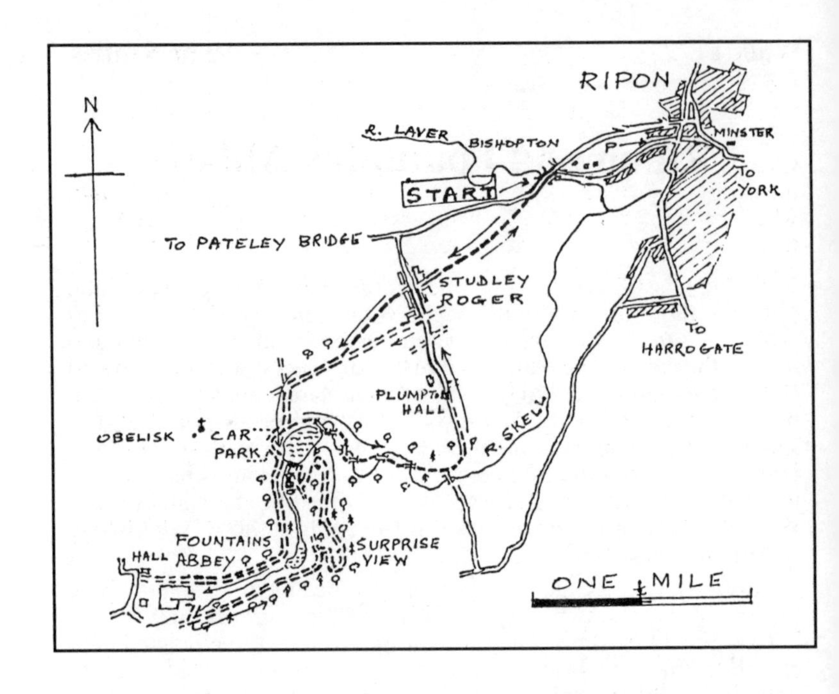

which supports waterfowl and wild life, crossing a cattle grid to make for the gate house and restaurant.

Motorists intending to do the shorter walk will park their cars here, having passed through the village of Studley Roger and the park gates beyond. The abbey grounds are open daily at 9.30 a.m.; closing is at 4 p.m. in winter months, 9 p.m. in summer, 5.30 p.m. in March, April and October, and 7 p.m. in May and September. From November to January, the opening time on Sundays is limited to 2-4 p.m. There is no admission on Christmas Eve, Christmas Day and Boxing Day.

From the gate, keep to the main drive, although one may wander at will. The route suggested here is one of many, but do not miss the abbey itself and the surprise view. Pass beautifully kept trees and water gardens in the Italian style, lovely lawns and landscaping conforming to the terrritory, and wildflowers in profusion from snowdrops onwards according to season. Rounding the bend, the noble ruin of the largest Cistercian abbey in Europe comes into sight. Situated in the tree-lined valley of the river Skell, it could not be in a more beautiful setting.

After you have explored the abbey and perhaps the hall (built in the reign of James I) and the twelfth century gate house, return to the east end of the ruin and cross to the other side of the valley on a track over the river. Turn sharply left to return on a wide track through trees, which soon comes down to the riverside where it is pleasant to wander by calm waters and weirs. At a sharp bend, where the water becomes a lake, look out for a white stone from which a track goes uphill to the right. Take it and, after it has swept around to the left near the top, you will see a summer-house. Here is the surprise view where you may take your fill of its beauty and regain your breath.

Continue along the top on a woodland trail, passing another summer-house on the left (or its foundations, for it was dismantled when last visited but, from appearances, was to be rebuilt). Occasional glimpses of the grounds below on the left and another lake on the right may be seen through the trees. On reaching another folly, go downhill on the left and through a tunnel just beyond it, emerging on the lawns of the water gardens. A palladian temple is on the left. Turn right, following the water, now in the form of a canal, to the weir which gushes on to the lake first seen earlier in the day. Here cross the substantial stepping stones back to the gate house and down to the lake shore, wandering to the lower end and passing over a footbridge.

Turn left and in the delectable little valley of the river Skell — now on your left — go downstream, crossing five stone footbridges. This valley is still in the deer park, but after crossing the fifth bridge the boundary wall is reached. Go through a gate in a high fence and immediately over a stile to continue down-valley through private woods, on a track carrying a right-of-way, near the end of which you will see on your right a wooden footbridge over the river. This could lead to an alternative way back to Ripon, but for today's journey do not cross it. Keep straight on, on the left bank, on a track which soon bears away to the left through the wood, emerging on the left side of a field, across which are clear views of Ripon dominated by the minster. Beyond it, across the Plain of York, are the Hambleton Hills.

On a cart track, pass Plumpton Hall Farm, where the track becomes a tarmac road. Soon the gates to Studley Royal Park are reached. Long route walkers continue to the village; short route walkers turn left along the drive to the car park. Continuing the long route, pass through the village as far as the cross tracks which will be recognised. Turn right at the signpost for Ripon, and retrace your steps.

Ilton Temple

TODAY'S walk is only short, but it could be combined with Walk 3, or with a fine motor ride on the narrow road over the moors to Lofthouse in Nidderdale (via Leighton), or a visit to Masham, with its air of repose, dignified houses, lovely old church with a spire and spacious marketplace. Near Masham is Swinton Park, the home of the Earl of Swinton, and on the Swinton estate, between Ilton and Healey, is a pseudo druidical temple, worth a visit itself and for the fine viewpoint nearby. The building of the temple provided occupation for tenants and estate workmen early in the nineteenth century during a time of distress. The temple lies in Druid's Plantation, to the west of the Ilton/Healey road. A 'No Through Road' sign marks the end of Knowle Lane, leading to the temple. A Forestry Commission sign shows F.R.P. No. 2, and another 'Jervaulx Forest — Druids' Wood.'

If all members of the party intend to walk 3½ miles there is no need to take the car further, but at the end of the lane is a fine car park and picnic place, laid out with benches and litter bags. If you prefer to leave the temple to the end of the journey, it should not be difficult to reverse the proposed route, but those intending to follow the clockwise journey as shown on the map go through the gate beside the main gate. Immediately in front is a notice which reads: 'Footpath to Druids' Temple by invitation of the Swinton Estate and Forestry Commission.' You could save a quarter of a mile by going straight ahead on the hard road; or you could make more of a walk of it by taking the alternative route left, which circles round to the viewpoint, marked by upright stones. Here one can see Leighton Reservoir, supplying water for Leeds; Colsterdale is beyond it; and on the skyline is Great Haw, with Little Haw to the right of it and another Little Haw (or South Haw) on the left.

Turn right to visit the temple, which is in sight, comprising an ovoid of stones with upright stones in the middle, a circle and a tomb. The twelve signs of the zodiac are portrayed on the high structure on the hill. To continue along the gravel road would return you to the picnic place. Those going further should take the wide green track forward on the left. Bear left at the first cross tracks on a path covered with pine needles, soon reaching the edge of the wood, with open views on the right of the Hambleton Hills. Continue to the gate at the opposite side of the wood; from here, keep to the

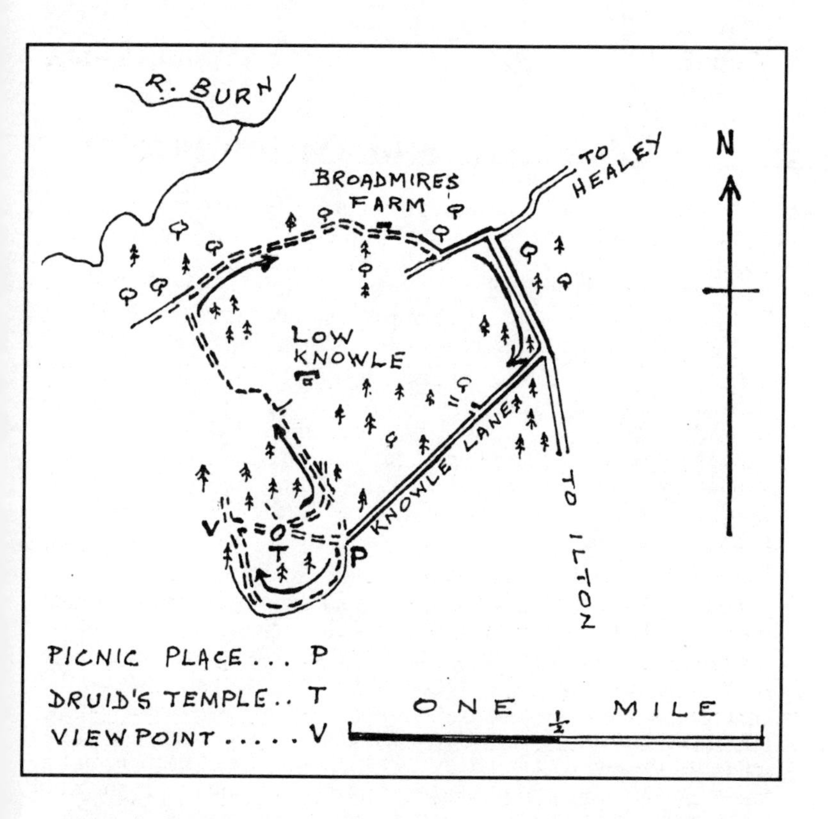

trees in the same line of march to come to an opening in the narrow belt of woodland (through which a cart track passes to Low Knowle Farm). Keep going down hill and, after about a hundred yards, join a tractor trail steeply swooping to a gate. Continue through a gap in the next hedge to the wood at the bottom of the hill, turn right, pass through a gateway at the bottom right-hand corner of the field, and follow a tractor trail through green pastures.

On the left is the valley of the river Burn; across the dale the village of Healey. Pass to the right of the buildings of Broadmores Farm, joining the farm road out to the narrow tarred road by a wood side, and take the next turn to the right to bring you back to the car at one end of Knowle Lane or the other.

Walk 3 8½ or 6½ miles

Colsterdale and Witton Fell

THE many charming features of Colsterdale are not so well known as they should be. It was famous in the First World War for the training camp of the Leeds Pals, the 15th Battalion, West Yorkshire Regiment, who on 1st July, 1916, suffered crippling casualties in the first Battle of the Somme. The camp was situated near Breary Bank, on the other side of the river from today's starting point.

Leave the car at Gollinglith Foot, near a telephone box beside the delectable river Burn, reached from Masham through Healey on the Colsterdale road. Those wishing to do the shorter version of the walk should continue up valley to get as near as possible to Slipstone Crags for a simple outward walk to Witton Fell and return as described below. Motorists approaching from Wensleydale or the north could use the alternative start from Stark Bank, near Ellerstring.

Leaving the riverside, walk up the track signposted to Low Agra, passing to the left of farm buildings and through a gate. Continue on the stony track through pasture and, after passing through a gate near Low Agra, keep near the boundary wall of the woods on the right to a gate in the wall between two plantations. Go straight up on good grass and make for the top left corner of the field. Agra Farm is away on your right. On a cart-way keep to the edge of a small conifer wood, towards the end of which go through an opening in the wall on your left and turn half right in the field to a gate in the cross wall. Now in an expansive pasture, make to the left of a single pine tree for a gate in the wall beyond, reaching a depression before it, where a clear track takes you to a foot-bridge and up to the gate. Leighton Reservoir can be seen on the right.

Continue in the line of march through heather on a faint track which, after passing marshy ground in a dip, eventually leads to the wall on the left — the parish boundary — let into which are several boundary stones. The first stone reached bears 'Mashamshire' on the near side and 'East Witton' on the far. Just beyond it, go over a wooden stile, turn right and continue alongside the boundary wall, where the right-of-way goes straight down to the Ellingstring road. Two tracks on the left, not marked on the map as rights-of-way at the time of writing, lead respectively to Moor Cote Farm and Stark Bank top, to which the tarred road from Ellingstring also leads. Below is the river Ure with Jervaulx on this side of it and Thornton Steward on the other. Away to the right, over the Vale of Mowbray, are the Hambleton Hills with the Clevelands to the north of them.

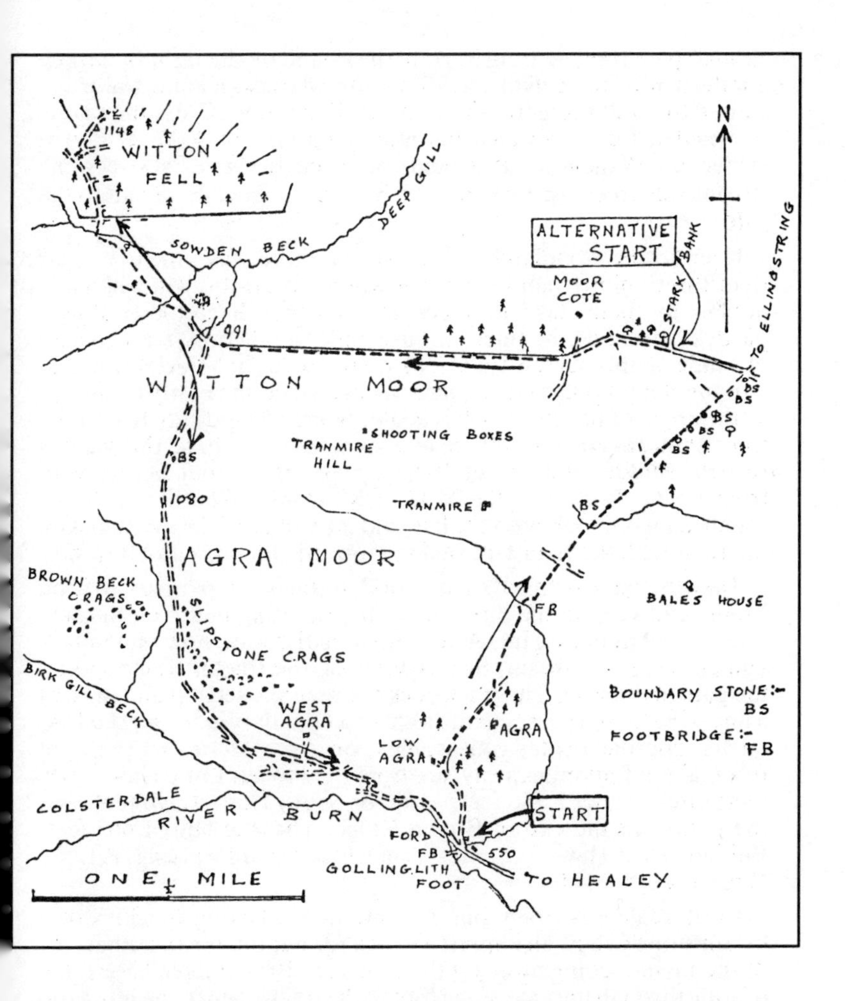

Join the metalled farm road leaving the corner of the tarmac road — the alternative starting point — and follow the main track past Moor Cote Farm, with its chalet roof. At the gate near the trees bear right on a well marked moorland track (sometimes muddy) with a conifer plantation on the right. The tree-covered objective of Witton Fell soon comes into sight to the right front, and when the view to the right opens out Leyburn can be seen across Wensleydale.

Coming down to a dip with a stream at the bottom, note a track to the left opposite a gate. We shall return to this point after climbing steadily to the top of Witton Fell, a mile away. Crossing the stream, the track soon leaves the side of the wall and makes for an isolated stunted pine tree; nearing it, go to the pound on the right (guarding a waterworks stop valve) and follow animal tracks leading towards a gate in the wall protecting Witton Fell Plantation. Cross the ravine of Sowden Beck — which become Deep Gill Beck lower down, visited on Walk 4 — at a point opposite the gate, above some stream-side trees. A track through bracken and heather leads to the gate.

Keep to the woodland ride as far as a three-way junction. Bear right for no more than forty yards where on the left you will find a narrow footpath; take it. Trees have recently been blown down, partly obstructing the track, so care must be taken. After a quarter of a mile on this narrow track look on the right for a track leading to a triangulation pillar fifteen yards away, which can easily be missed as the angle of the side track is acute. Some 85 yards further on the trees thin out on the left, above some crags, where the view is superb. Middle and Lower Wensleydale stretch out before you, from Castle Bolton to the Vale of Mowbray. Another castle — Middleham — is below on the left; and the village of East Witton is on the right with the river Ure snaking towards Jervaulx and beyond.

Take the same path out of the wood, retracing steps across Witton Moor, and keep in the direction of the shooting house on the sky-line — on Tranmire Hill. After rejoining the wall, now on the left, and crossing the stream, turn right along the tractor trail opposite the gate in the wall. The track goes between the second and third of a line of butts and passes to the right of a boundary stone marked 'A' on the approach side; you are now on Agra Moor. To the right front, about four miles away, are from right to left Little Haw, 1,639 feet; Great Haw, 1,786 feet; Little or South Haw, 1,596 feet: and the pimple at the end of Brown Ridge, Throstle Hill, 1,562 feet. Behind Great Haw, 7½ miles from where we are walking, is Little Whernside, 1,984 feet.

Colsterdale now opens out in front, the track going quickly down by Slipstone Crags, an impressive rock formation. On the other side of the ravine, going away on the right, are Brown Beck Crags. On passing through the gate at the foot of the track keep to the left-hand green track by the wall on your left, on springy turf beside bracken and gorse. Join the road leading from West Agra Farm. Below are large pipes crossing the river Burn taking water from the catchment area to Leighton Reservoir and, eventually, to Leeds. The reservoir is on the other side of the hill behind the red house seen ahead. The road takes a sharp bend down to the river at a gate marked 'Boddy Close'. Those electing to do the shorter return journey may choose to leave the car here. A pleasant stroll down the road, or round the bends of the river, brings one back to Gollinglith Foot.

Walk 4 **Route A: 9 miles; B: 6 miles; C: 4 miles; D: 2 miles**

Jervaulx Abbey and the River Ure

JERVAULX is situated on the main road to Wensleydale from Ripon, 5½ miiles from Masham and 3½ from Middleham., The Cistercian abbey was founded by monks who came to the site from Fors in 1147. They bred horses and were reputed to have discovered the recipe for making Wensleydale cheese. Only the outline of the thirteenth century church remains, built up of stones from the other parts of the abbey. The twelfth century lay brothers' range is still to be seen; also the fourteenth century abbot's lodge, fifteenth century infirmary, chapter house and cloister. The buildings and grounds, privately owned, are open to the public on weekdays from 10 a.m. to 6 p.m.

Park the car in the car park opposite the abbey. Those wishing to walk on routes A, B or C go downhill along the main road for 300 yards and, immediately after passing over Lea Gill Beck, turn right on a tractor trail by the side of the stream which soon leads to the river Ure — broad, fast-flowing, stony in parts and often tree-lined. The path to the left all the way to Cover Bridge is easily followed by the riverside, passing a fish pond on the left and Danby Park on the other side of the river. It is pleasant to linger by the weir beside Danby Low Mill, now disused, and to observe the first of three tree-covered islands called The Batts. Passing through a gate the track is now beside the river Cover, narrower and swifter than the Ure, leading to the shapely Cover Bridge. The Inn, quaint and popular with fishermen, was established in 1674. Route C walkers are recommended to return here along the riverside, the main road being further and more dangerous.

Routes A and B walkers cross the road, descend five stone steps and immediately cross two stiles to come again to the river Cover. Continue walking beside it on the outside of a fence, make for a gap in the hedge ahead and go through a gate in the next hedge. Cut across the field to a barn, at the far side of which is a 'V' stile in the field wall. Turn left at the other side. Keep the wall on your left all the way to the foot of the hill below East Witton. Do not go through the gate on the left, but continue forward over a stile, the boundary on your immediate left now being a fence and hedge. Enter a small field, leaving it by a stile in the far left-hand corner. Pass through a paddock and arrive at the village through a small gate on the right of the Methodist chapel.

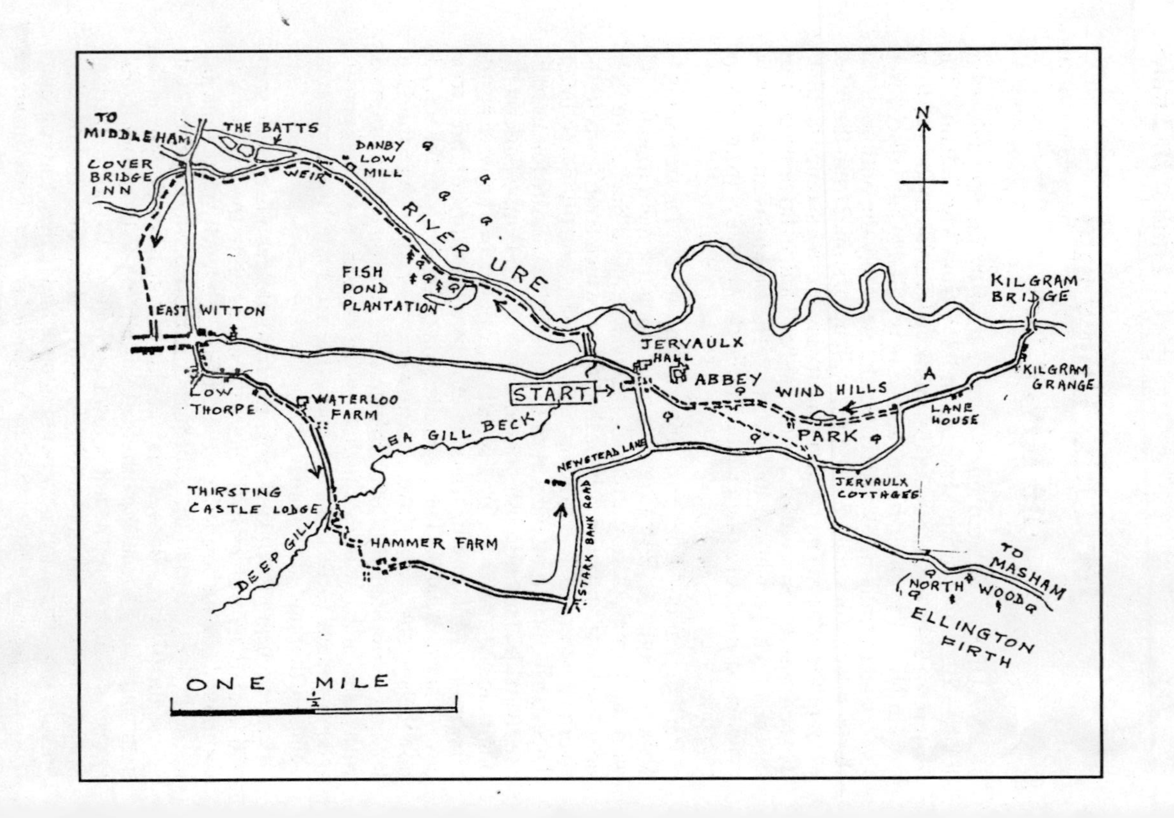
TO MIDDLEHAM
THE BATTS
COVER BRIDGE INN
DANBY LOW MILL
WEIR
RIVER URE
N
FISH POND PLANTATION
EAST WITTON
KILGRAM BRIDGE
JERVAULX HALL
ABBEY
KILGRAM GRANGE
A
WIND HILLS
START
LANE HOUSE
LOW THORPE
WATERLOO FARM
LEA GILL BECK
PARK
NEWSTEAD LANE
JERVAULX COTTAGES
THIRSTING CASTLE LODGE
STARK BANK ROAD
DEEP GILL
HAMMER FARM
TO MASHAM
NORTH WOOD
ELLINGTON FIRTH
ONE MILE
½

East Witton comprises an elongated green with roads on each side and neat, regular cottages. Turn left towards the church but, on reaching the main road, take the narrow road on the right through Low Thorpe, bearing left at the fork. Pass the graveyard of the former St Martin's church and go to the right of Waterloo Farm and its blue silo. Keep to the tarmac road on a sharp, uphill climb at the top of which, beyond Thirsting Castle Lodge — where the dogs will bark — the tarmac expires. The track goes over a rushing stream, Deep Gill Beck on the right which becomes Lea Gill Beck on the left, and into a field.

Leave the field by a gate near the top right-hand corner, taking a zig-zag track uphill. At the end of the first 'zig' the track forks — take the right-hand track to a post and wire fence, turn left and take the first gate on the right, keeping a double fence on your left. Go through two gates in quick succession on your left and make for the right-hand side of Hammer Farm, picking up the farm road in front of the house. After passing over a stream on a cattle grid, the farm road goes into a lane which leads to the narrow, tarmac Stark Bank Road. Turn left on the road which leads down to Newstead Lane and out on to the main road. Route B walkers turn left here and you will soon be back at Jervaulx.

Route A walkers, instead of returning to the car park, turn right and walk on the busy main road (single file on the right-hand side recommended) for a little more than half a mile. Jervaulx Abbey Park is on the left. Where the main road turns right for Masham, opposite the park gate, keep straight on, passing Jervaulx Cottages and, now on a minor road, continue to Kilgram Bridge said by some writers to be the eastern boundary of Wensleydale. It is a fine bridge, over the wide river Ure, with a raised trod above flood level at the far side.

Return along this minor road as far as the lodge on the right at a bend. A sign tells you the drive is a private road, but there is a right of way for walkers on the road through the park, hilly with drumlins (glacial deposits) and well laid out with clumps of trees. Pass a lake and a small pond, observe the abbey on the right, and leave the grounds by the footpath to a signpost by the roadside. The car park is almost opposite.

Strollers on route D should go into the park at the signpost (which reads 'to the Abbey') and take the main drive until nearly opposite the fine house, Abbey Hill, on the right. Take the footpath leading to the gates near Jervaulx Cottages; turn left on the road to follow Kilgram Lane as far as the lodge on the left; and go over the cattle grid and into the park as described above. The right of way through the park applies only to the two routes mentioned. All other tracks are private.

Walk 5 **6 miles**

Great Haw

COVERDALE, the lovely valley of the river Cover (to rhyme with 'hover'), offers many good walks, up hill and down dale. The intention today is to climb a gentle thousand feet — or nearly so. The charming ride along the narrow Braithwaite Lane from East Witton takes one past Coverham Bridge. On the other side of the river is Coverham Abbey, now a farm with little left to see of the old monastery. Do not cross the bridge but continue by car to West Scrafton where there is a parking place on the road side just before the houses.

On entering the village there is a bridge over the rushing stream of Great Gill with a gate by the side of it. Go uphill with the stream on your right and a modernised country house on your left. The track soon leaves the beck and curls uphill on the right-hand side of a wall ceasing to be in somewhat muddy condition and becoming a smooth green track through tufted grass, never more than 100 yards from the wall until this turns away and our track turns right, sloping uphill. Before taking this turn note the crags ahead with an anvil shaped stone on top — Great Roova.

Walking up the long but gradual slope, notice across the marshy ground on the right a cleft in the moor, showing the line of the return journey. Pass an automatic ram for pumping water on the left and, a little further on, Roova Pot Hole fifty feet uphill (and therefore to be searched for). Next come spoil heaps from some old, small, drift coal mines — narrow seams of coal were mined in the Dales, chiefly in the late eighteenth and early nineteenth centuries.

Cross a small stream, headed by Great Bank Well; the path is reduced to a single track going on to a deep gully with a natural bridge over the stream. If you reach this point you have been led beyond the official track, which you can soon regain by following the stream upwards to the big spoil heap, enclosed by a fence protecting animals — and you — from the wide circular shaft of a coal mine. The lip of the shaft is crumbly and insecure — so be warned! Between the mine and a post and wire fence, seen ahead, is some rather boggy ground. Cross this to a gate in the fence where we leave the right of way to turn right, following the parish boundary which can be seen stretching from Great and Little Roova Crags, on the left, to our objective today, on the right, to and beyond it. Animal tracks go through the tufted grass on our side of the fence, and through the heather on the other. From here, in clear weather, the 'table top' of Little Whernside can be seen to the right front, as we advance, with Great Whernside going away from it.

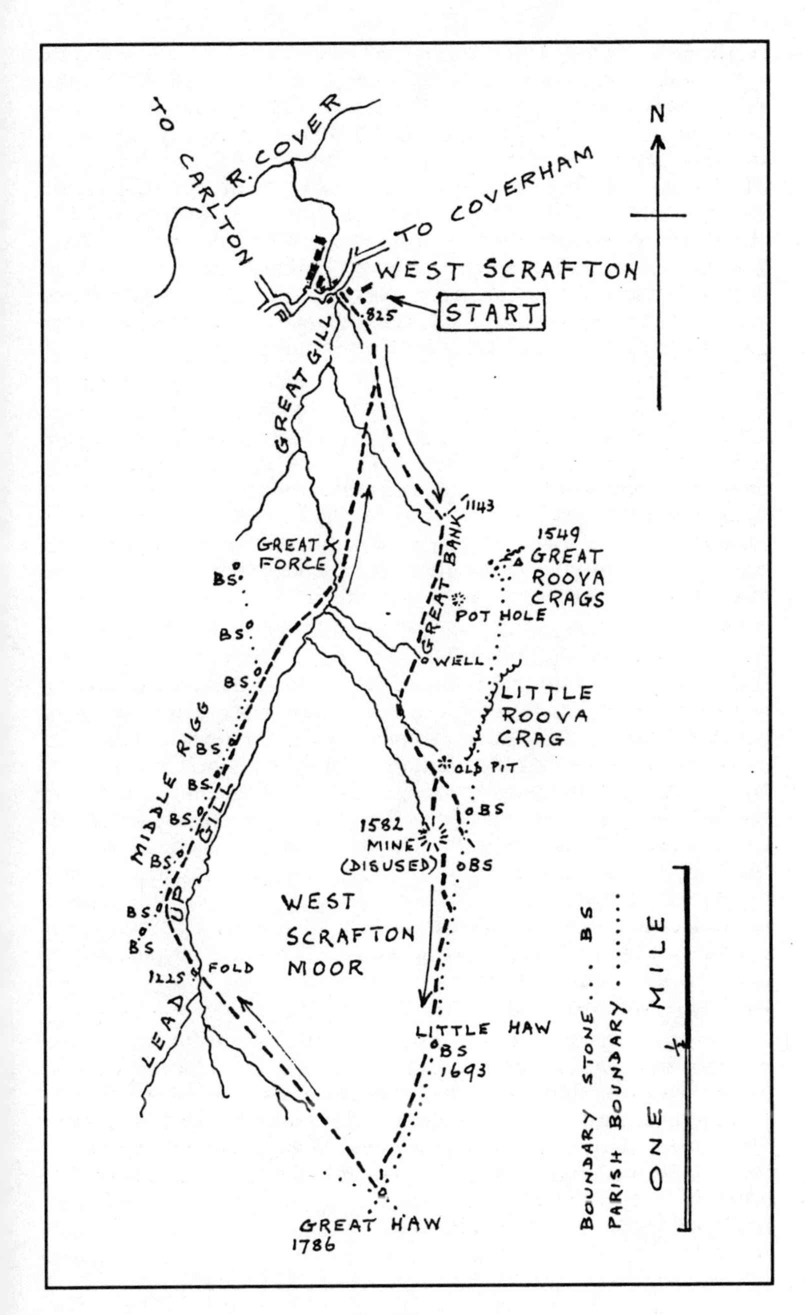
TO CARLTON
R. COVER
TO COVERHAM
N
WEST SCRAFTON
START
825
GREAT GILL
1143
GREAT BANK
1549
GREAT ROOYA CRAGS
GREAT FORCE
POT HOLE
WELL
LITTLE ROOVA CRAG
OLD PIT
MIDDLE RIGG
UP GILL
BS
1582
MINE (DISUSED)
WEST SCRAFTON MOOR
1225
FOLD
LEAD
LITTLE HAW
1693
GREAT HAW
1786
BOUNDARY STONE ... BS
PARISH BOUNDARY ......
ONE ½ MILE

About half a mile from where the fence was joined, another gate is reached — on some slightly higher ground. Notice that one of the gateposts is a boundary stone; this is Little Haw. The gills starting from the moor top on the left go down into Colsterdale, and straight ahead is Great Haw. On the way to it there was once another gate, which was on the right of way we shall pick up on the return from the top, a quarter of a mile further on, where our fence meets the fence of the old county boundary. A boundary stone will be seen where this gate stood, with the words 'Danby-Mashamshire' inscribed on it. For views of Nidderdale it is necessary to con-tinue in the line of march on the other side of the fence. The boundary to the left front goes down to the other Little Haw (or South Haw).

Retrace your steps from the fence junction for about a quarter of a mile and then bear to the left at an angle of about 50 degrees to the fence towards the right-hand nick of two which should be seen at the edge of the moor. Although there is a right of way (from Nidderdale) there is no well-trodden footpath on the top of the moor. Animal tracks should, however, help to take you through the tufted grass towards the moor edge (this is West Scrafton Moor), but leave the track which continues along the edge so as to reach the brow of the moor at a point just to the right of a gill.

Down below you should see a sheep fold, immediately below the junction of Lead Up Gill and the side beck. Go to it. Descending, the grass becomes smooth beneath the feet but on reaching bracken you should with luck find a grassy path down to the stream. Cross it before coming to the fold and you will soon pass the foundations of an old building — marked 'shooting house' on the 2½ inch map. Now there is a path going up to the boundary fence on the left — on the Middle Rigg — from which there are views of the length of Coverdale on the left with the two Whernsides at its head. Follow the line of boundary stones until they bear off to the left. At this point make for the stream which is crossed within a hundred yards of the wall end. It can be pleasant to linger here, where the water falls over a series of little ledges — although a few hundred yards lower down is the more dramatic Great Force, the second of two waterfalls, well worth making one of the objectives of this walk.

The official track takes a short sharp pull up from the stream crossing and levels off, gradually moving away from the beck across ground — sometimes marshy — between two walls, eventually joining the outward track which runs alongside the right-hand wall. On the left, across Coverdale, is Penhill which will be climbed on Walk 6. To the left of Penhill is Harland Hill which will be encircled on Walk 7. Less than 500 yards of descent, after joining the outward track, brings you back to West Scrafton.

Walk 6 **3 miles**

Penhill

TRAVELLERS in the Vale of Mowbray or on the Hambleton Hills must often have looked to the west to identify Wensleydale by its jaws, especially the southern 'jaw,' Penhill — a miniature Ingleborough — bounded by Coverdale, Walden, and Wensleydale.

The plan for today is a simple one, put in especially for those who like to get on the tops without too much exertion! The more energetic could quite easily combine it with Walk 7 by using the parish boundary over the Height of Hazely, the west height of Penhill, but it should be remembered that the right of way stops opposite Black Scar. The short journey is to the Beacon, 1,685 feet above sea level — but the start will be from 1,175 feet. On the narrow road between West Witton and Melmerby is a cattle grid where the enclosed road goes on to Middleham High Moor (which provides the summer gallops for racehorses from many stables). A hundred yards downhill from the cattle grid is a gateway on the Penhill side of the road and a wide grass verge on which to park. There is also a convenient parking area just above the cattle grid.

From the gateway there is a track, which keeps to the brow of the hill through fields and a number of gates, heading straight for the Beacon visible at the top of Penhill. Take it, and emerging from the fields on to the moor you should see on your right, from right to left: the village of Wensley in a lovely setting; Bolton Hall and parkland; Preston-under-Scar, suitably named; Redmire; and Castle Bolton above and to the left, with the distinctive shape of Bolton Castle beyond the village. Passing through a moorland gate, the track takes on a new shape with ditches on each side. It curves round to the left of the steep hillside and 200 yards further on reaches a thorn tree a few feet below on the left, marking Robin Hood's Well which exudes clear refreshng water. It is easy to miss the thorn tree, so do not rely on this as a convenient waymark. Continue upwards on the track for about 100 yards and then turn right across the moat to scramble up the square stone cairn which marks the site of the Beacon. One can imagine a fire being lit here when news was received of the defeat of the Spanish Armada. West Witton can now be seen below in Wensleydale, while on the other side, looking across Coverdale, on the left is Witton Moor (not unlike Penhill), then come Little and Great Haw and over to the right are Little and Great Whernside.

Take the green track through tufted grass and heather, keeping to the Wensleydale edge of the moor — the caravans below tend to

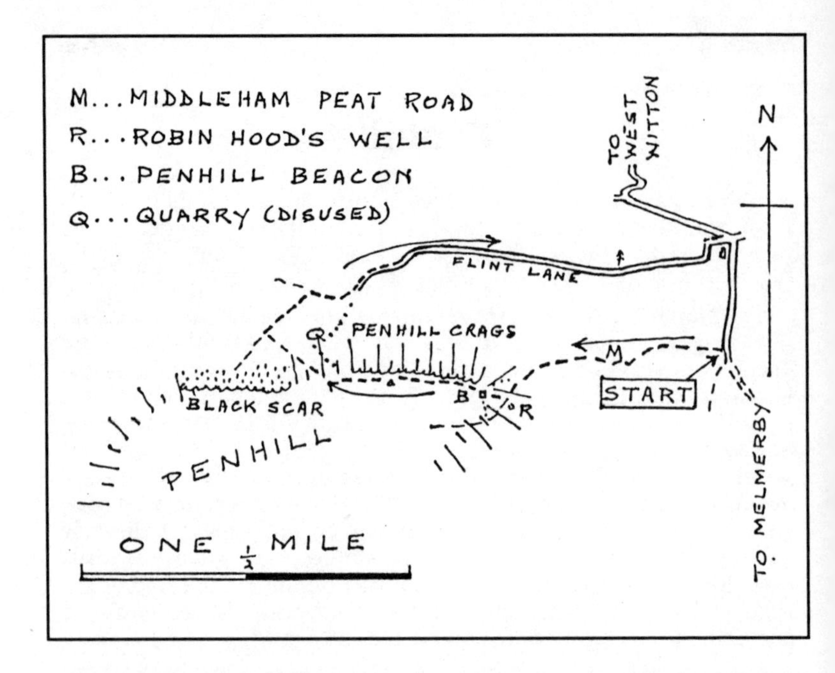

spoil the picture, but the site is well concealed from the main road and West Witton village. Pass to the right of a round barrow, with an upright stone on top, and along the top of the tall Penhill Crags as far as a slit stile in a wall across the path. Those who do not seek a scramble down the grassy slope between Penhill Crags and Black Scar, which can be dangerous in winter weather, may consider returning to the car from here by making an about turn. Another complication is that although we intend to join a right of way down below, the link between is open ground with no public path shown on the map.

Continuing beyond the stile, the shapely form of Addlebrough can be seen ahead on the other side of Bishopdale. After negotiating a wire fence — the wire near the wall on the right is not barbed — walk for 100 yards or so along the cliff edge. The crags end here and the steep grass slope can be descended to join tracks among old workings and through a pasture to a gate at the right-hand bottom corner. Turn right at the other side and walk on the left of a wall to another gate which leads to the walled Flint Lane — a green lane from which there are more good views of Wensleydale. This in turn joins the narrow tarmac road above West Witton. Turn right and walk uphill to the starting point.

Walk 7 **9¼ miles**

Coverdale and Walden

USING two ancient bridleways between the lovely valleys of Coverdale and Walden, the walker completely encircles Harland Hill — an extension of Penhill — and climbs fairly gently to heights giving fine vistas of the surrounding country. The walk may begin either from Cote Bridge in Walden, or if one finds oneself in Coverdale, from half a mile west of Carlton. Let us start from the former, taking us through the well-kept village of West Burton, which has some fine houses, a compact green and a delightful waterfall. At the top of the village, bear left in the car, passing the 'No Through Road' sign and taking the road for Walden South. Go gently over the hump-back Cote Bridge, where there is a caravan site, and park on the wide verge or on the triangle of grass 200 yards beyond the bridge.

Walk up the stony track, passing to the left of a square chimney. To regain breath, pause at the first gate to look back. Beyond Walden is Bishopdale, and further west Addlebrough stands above the general line of the hills. The village on the other side of Wensleydale is Carperby, with some of the easterly houses of Aysgarth in between. Past the end of a wall the stony track turns temporarily to the right; either keep to it or cut off a corner by going forward up the hill. Do not be tempted to the track by the fence lower down on the left, but make the stiffish climb through bracken, bearing right until the track — now green and cropped — is regained. The path clings more or less to a stone wall on the left, but leave this when it turns away and continue in the same direction — or slightly to the right to avoid some marshy ground.

Very soon you will see the parish boundary wall. Turn left on a green double track before it, crossing the line of march, and right after a few yards on a single track which soon becomes double. Go through a gateway in the boundary wall, turn immediately to the right and, after a few yards, bear left and follow a double green track crossing enclosed land. Now we are looking into Coverdale; the track reaches the wall on the right and keeps to it until passing out of the enclosure at a gap in the next wall. Keep straight forward on a green track, going downhill parallel to a gill on the left. As Howden Lodge comes into sight, take stock of the hills on the other side of Coverdale, from Witton Fell on the left past Roova Crags, Little and Great Haw, to Little Whernside on the right — Great Whernside will also soon come into view.

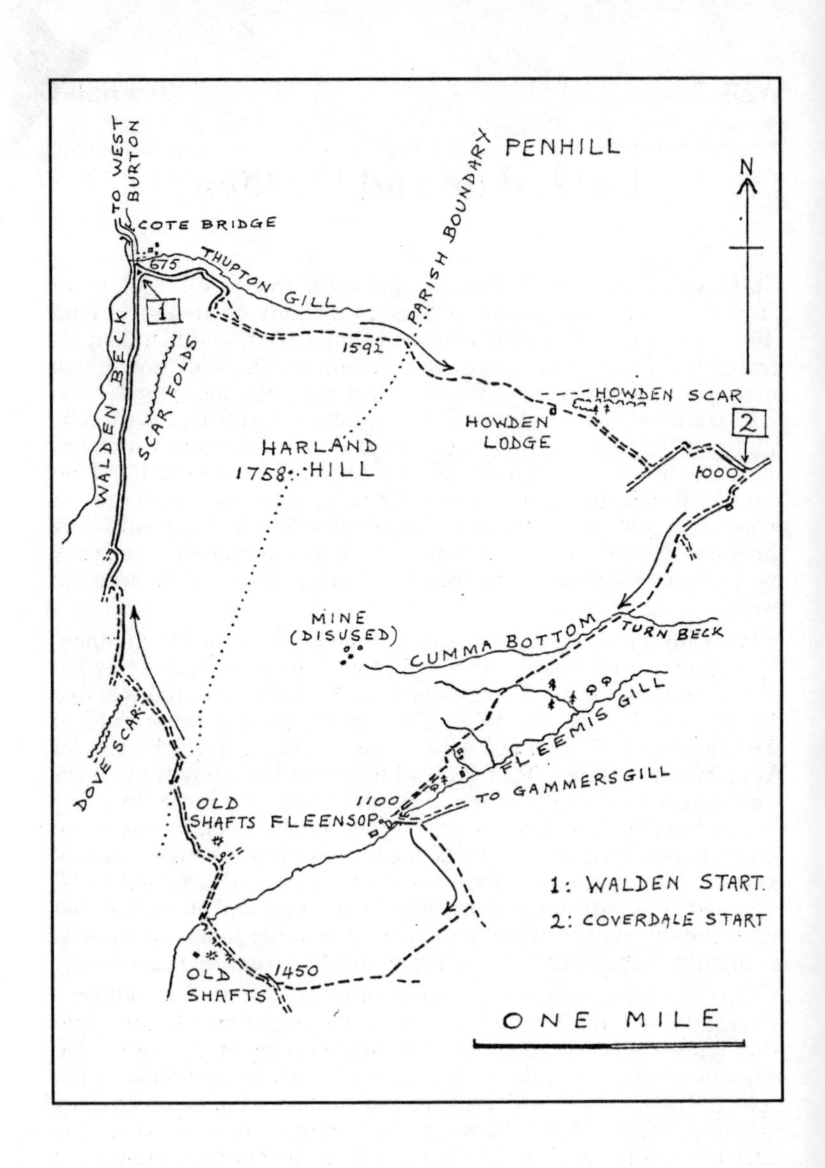
PENHILL
N
TO WEST BURTON
COTE BRIDGE
675
THUPTON GILL
PARISH BOUNDARY
1
WALDEN BECK
SCAR FOLDS
1592
HOWDEN SCAR
HOWDEN LODGE
2
HARLAND HILL
1758
1000
MINE (DISUSED)
CUMMA BOTTOM
TURN BECK
FLEEMIS GILL
DOVE SCAR
TO GAMMERSGILL
OLD SHAFTS
FLEENSOP
1100
1: WALDEN START.
2: COVERDALE START
OLD SHAFTS
1450
ONE MILE

Pass immediately to the left of the now deserted house; the deep drift on the left is Howden Scar. Keeping Howden Scar on your left, join a tractor trail along a line of shooting butts — a green, heathery, gravelly track which brings you to two gates at the junction of walls. Take the left-hand one, turning squarely; go through another gate on to a green track between a wall and a barbed wire fence, and continue downhill on a track between walls which meets a narrow tarmac road. Turn right through a metal gate.

People starting from Coverdale should leave the car here on the wide grass verge, having taken the narrow uphill road, marked 'unsuitable for motors.' out of the top end of the village of Carlton. It turns left to go up the dale; park at the end of the tarred road. The road is still shown as untarred in the current editions of O.S. maps. Walk through the gate straight ahead.

On a good farm road go through a wooden gate, passing in front of the farm, and then an iron gate beyond. The road turns left in the direction of another farm but go straight on, passing through a wooden gate and keeping a wall on your left. Go through a second gate and then a gap — often muddy — in a wall. Step across a tributary of Turn Beck and then through a gate immediately beyond. Turn right, keeping the wall on your right; when you reach the end of this wall look for a gate ahead and pass through it. Go down to Turn Beck, crossing it over stepping stones to a gate. Bear to the right along the depression of an ancient track following the stream in which there is a succession of pleasant little waterfalls. By keeping just above stream level you see ahead a gate — go through it.

The hollow to the right front is Cumma Bottom. Underfoot the grass is tufted; on the left is a conifer plantation — keep about 200 yards away from it in order to be on the right of way and to dodge a depression ahead. When you reach a wall across your path you have a problem. The official footpath passes through it 200 yards from the edge of the wood but when last visited there were no signs of gap, gate or stile — and the wall has many loose stones in it. This can be overcome by going down to the copse (off the right-of-way), crossing the wall using a step stone in the corner and passing through a gate about 150 yards along another wall (on your left). Cross the next field diagonally to join a farm road which takes you through the next plantation, regaining the right of way. Continue to a tarmac road just in front of Fleensop Farm house. Turn left over a bridge, and 300 yards later go through a gate set at an angle on the right.

Do not stay too long on the cart road in the field but go uphill to a gate in the top left-hand corner. On the open moor keep to the right of a wall, veering away from it when you see a post on the ridge by the side of another wall. A notice says 'Bridle road to Walden . . .';

we follow this to the right, leaving the Horsehouse bridle road. Keep the wall on your left for just under a mile until, opposite a stile, turn half right away from it on a clear track. Pass a white-topped post — and another one — before reaching a wall across the path which bears to the right to a green gate.

Turn right on a double track on the other side and pass some old coal mines. Going down to the stream, look to the right for a good view of Fleemis Gill which was crossed at Fleensop. Notice, in dry weather, that the water of the beck disappears into the ground at the foot of a waterfall. Keep to the main track on the other side and go through a gate; at a fork a guide post indicates the way, bearing left to West Burton and Aysgarth (it also shows we are on the Horsehouse bridleway). Look to the left for Buckden Pike coming into sight; then go through another gate in the boundary wall (passed earlier in the day on the other side of Harland Hill). Descending into Walden, the hill on the other side of the dale is Wasset Fell. Pass through another gate and by the side of an old railway luggage van to join the narrow tarmac road at a signpost which indicates we have come from the direction of Horsehouse and Kettlewell and tells us the way to West Burton. A mile of walking on the quiet road above the delightful Walden Beck finishes the journey of those who elected to start from Cote Bridge.

Walk 8 **Route A: 6¼ miles**
Route B: 4½ miles

Walden Beck and Buckden Pike

BUCKDEN PIKE dominates the whole valley of Walden. It is one of the highest peaks in the Yorkshire Pennines but 'Pike' is a misnomer: its top is bulky but not sharp. Well-trodden tracks go over the fell from Wharfedale side — not all rights of way — but the ancient bridleway from Walden Head to Starbotton is not much walked upon these days, although we shall use it. Do not be deceived by the short distance; five hours could easily be taken over the longer journey, if time is allowed for rests and admiration of the views. It is not a casual stroll and walkers should be properly shod, clad and provisioned.

Walden Beck is delightful and well worth a visit — at least as far as the first waterfall — and one can return via Groove End if a little climbing is acceptable. Motor nearly to Walden Head via West Burton where one takes the 'No through road' and the turn to Walden North. The tarmac road ends at Kentucky House, the last farm on the left; just before it there is room for parking three or four cars on the grass verge. Continue on foot from here up the dale, past the farm, after which the road becomes a track crossing the stream on a wooden bridge.

Do not go over the stream but pass through a gateway on the left just before it, keeping by the stream side. Climb over a wall across the line of march near its junction with another wall on the other side — there is not a proper stile but the right of way is undoubted. Continue up this delectable quiet valley, with the burbling beck on the right and the hills ahead. A tractor trail leads slightly up the hillside, but never more than 50 yards from the stream, to a gate in a cross wall. On the other side of the stream is a plantation; go past the end of it for about 150 yards, crossing to the other side of the beck before reaching some cliffs. This should present no difficulty if the water is low, but if the stream is full do not make the attempt because the intention is to return to this side (the left side but the true right bank) a few hundred yards further along. Those who have forded the water join a green tractor trail on the valley floor, noting the position of the stream crossing for the return. Go over the Deepdale Beck on smooth rock and soon you will see that the main stream on the left has gone underground; here you can cross to a well-used sheep track on the other side and re-cross above the next junction to walk between two streams for a hundred yards or so.

Those intending to follow B route should return to this place after continuing upstream.

B walkers, having returned from seeing the first waterfall (the biggest and best), turn up the side valley at the end of which they will see steep cliffs. This little dale is also delightful. Before reaching the cliffs leave the stream side and climb up the hillside on the right to join the right of way at the top — on Groove End. Turn right on sheep tracks, which abound, and when presented with alternatives take the track on the right unless it is obviously going down into the valley. The right of way is over the hump of Groove End, rejoining the Deepdale Beck where it was crossed on the outward trip. Retrace your steps to your point of departure.

Route A walkers continue up the main gill, very soon reaching a series of rocky cascades, one drop being particularly impressive. Above the fall the water passes over some flat rocks and beneath the high crags of Raven Scar. Scramble up by the side of the beck, crossing and recrossing, until you come to the last of the falls. This one has less water going over it and is mossy. Climb up the drift on the left of the fall (as you face it); if you turn round and look back you see Brown Haw, 1,904 feet, part of North Moor. Above the waterfall the parish boundary fence may be seen on the skyline on the left; straight ahead, and to the right front, are signs of the old county boundary wall. These enclosures are somewhat comforting if one is caught in mist — the trail may be picked up by turning to the right on reaching one boundary or the other. Pit spoil heaps may also be seen towards the skyline to the right front; make for them, using water courses which are easier walking than the heather and tufted grass of the moor.

At the first division of water above the fall, take the main course on the left-hand side for a simple route to the pits. Look back, when the stream becomes merely a trickle, down the dale of Walden and beyond Brown Haw for a sight of Harland Hill and the back of Penhill. On the left-hand side of the valley is Noughtberry Hill. Looking east, notice the shape of Little Whernside — not such a tableland as when seen from the opposite direction. At the old quarries shelter can be found within carefully constructed walls. Here also is the unmistakable path of the right of way, which somewhat unusually is clearly seen. We shall pick it up later on, returning from the top, but its position may then have to be judged rather than seen.

From the quarries it is only a quarter of a mile to the county boundary wall across rough country. Make for it at its nearest point in order to join the beaten track by the side of the wall. Turn right on springy peat — Wharfedale and Littondale are below on the left; behind is Great Whernside, now seen as a continuation of Little

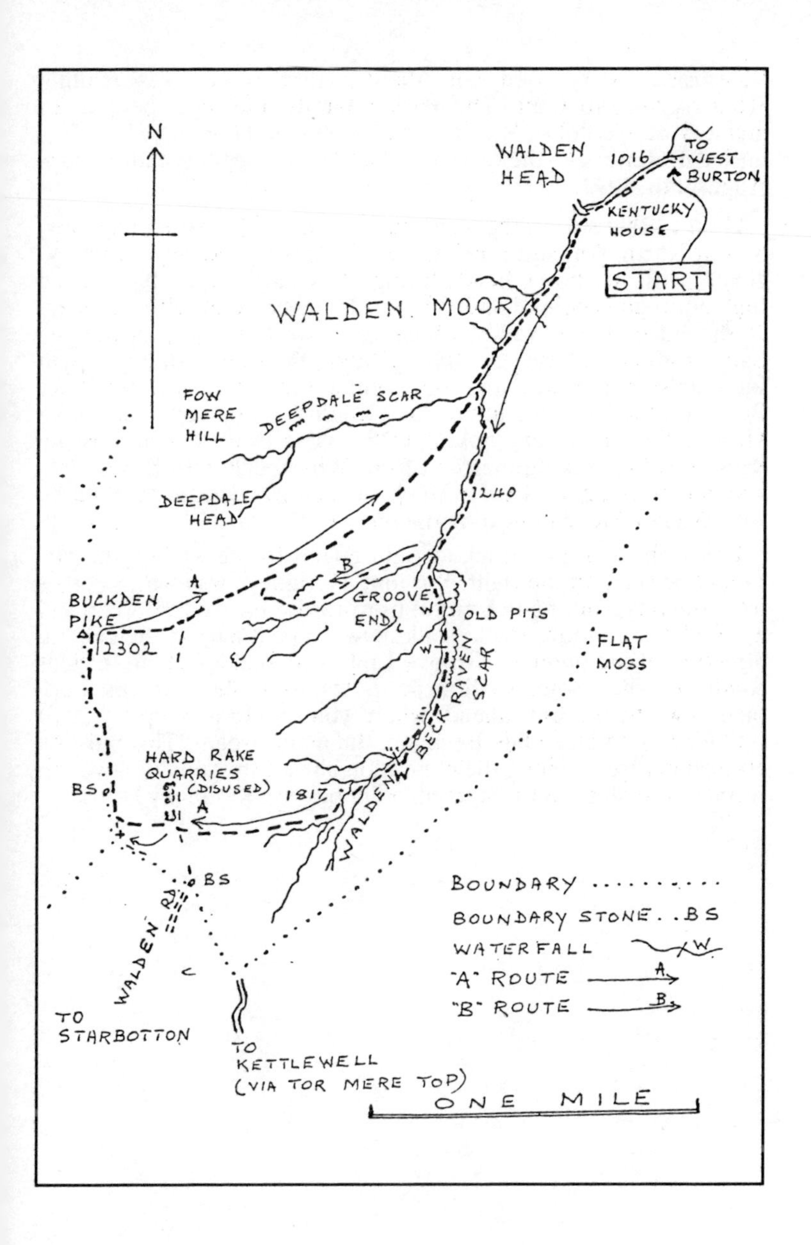
N
WALDEN HEAD
1016
TO WEST BURTON
KENTUCKY HOUSE
START
WALDEN MOOR
FOW MERE HILL
DEEPDALE SCAR
DEEPDALE HEAD
1240
B
A
BUCKDEN PIKE
2302
GROOVE END
W
OLD PITS
W
RAVEN SCAR
FLAT MOSS
WALDEN BECK
HARD RAKE QUARRIES (DISUSED)
BS
1817
A
BS
WALDEN RD
TO STARBOTTON
TO KETTLEWELL (VIA TOR MERE TOP)
BOUNDARY
BOUNDARY STONE . . BS
WATERFALL
W
"A" ROUTE
A
"B" ROUTE
B
ONE MILE

Whernside. Very soon you should come to a cross reading 'Thanksgiving to God. The Parker family and local people. In memory of five Polish R.A.F. airmen who died here on 31.1.42 — buried in Newark — the survivor.' The date at the foot of the cross is August 5th, 1973.

On the other side of the wall you are in the old West Riding, now part of North Yorkshire. From here there is a good view of Pen-y-ghent, with its 'lion's head' facing towards the left; flat-topped Ingleborough is behind and Whernside, less recognisable, appears at the head of the valley which goes away in front of you — Langstrothdale Chase. Continuing along the side of the wall, you soon arrive at the cairn and trig. point at the top of Buckden Pike. Below on the left is the minor road leading to the track over Stake Moss to Semer Water; looking in the same direction there is the Kidstones Pass taking the road from Wharfedale into Bishopdale and behind is a good view of the U-shaped glacial dale of Walden, with Walden Head indicating the point of return.

Leave the top on a track at right angles to the wall — the pits should be seen on the right. We join the right of way which comes from the pits, curving in front of us towards Groove End. You will not find a continuous track; walk between peat hags in the general direction of the bump of Groove End — or Walden Head in clear conditions. Pass some shallow pot holes, using sheep tracks dropping down to the spur ahead, where you should pick up a tractor trail leading to Deepdale Beck and the main stream. This must be crossed before reaching the plantation ahead, thus enabling you to retrace your steps to the starting point beyond Kentucky House.

Walk 9 **5 or 1½ miles**

Bolton Castle and Apedale

PROBABLY the most easily recognised feature in Wensleydale is the square keep of Bolton Castle; maybe the least-known is Apedale, so today we shall combine the two. The shorter walk involves motoring from the castle to the second guide post on the Grinton road and taking the walk along the rough track to Dent's Houses and back.

Quoting from *The Yorkshire Dales* by Marie Hartley and Joan Ingilby, 'Bolton Castle is owned by Lord Bolton, and is open to the public. It was built by Richard Scrope, first Lord Scrope, Chancellor of Englnd, who in 1379 obtained licence to crenellate his manor house; some details of its erection and construction are recorded by Leland. From 13th July 1568 to 26 January 1569 Mary Queen of Scots was imprisoned here. Besieged by the Parliamentarian forces in 1645, the castle capitulated, and was eventually dismantled. The N.E. tower fell in a storm in 1761, and in the early nineteenth century the S.W. tower and W. curtain were roofed. The castle, with square towers at the corners,and built round a rectangular courtyard, is one of the most interesting of its period.' The car park is at the west end of the village, just beyond the castle. Refreshments are served in the castle, which may be a factor in deciding whether or not to visit it at the beginning or the end of the walk.

Begin the walk by taking the road through the village and continue for three-quarters of a mile, passing the little dell of Apedale Beck, to the 'T' junction where the signpost reads 'Grinton 4½, Reeth 5½, Redmire ½.' Turn left uphill on the wide road; the road narrows and becomes much quieter beyond the quarry entrance. On to higher ground, you will see a short chimney — this is the old Cobscar smelt mill on Preston Moor. Apedale will shortly be visible on the left. Pass the first guide post, and leave the road at the second post half a mile further on, bearing left on to a stony track — the point at which those choosing to stroll into Apedale may leave the car.

The gradual descent into the valley reveals the shooting hut at Dent's Houses. Above and beyond are tracks leading to old mines where the spoil heaps are still to be seen but, having mellowed over the years, they are no longer a blot on the landscape. Up to the last century, the lead mining industry must have given Apedale a very different appearance from the quiet and remote scene now before us. The wide track snakes up the dale on the way to Crackpot in

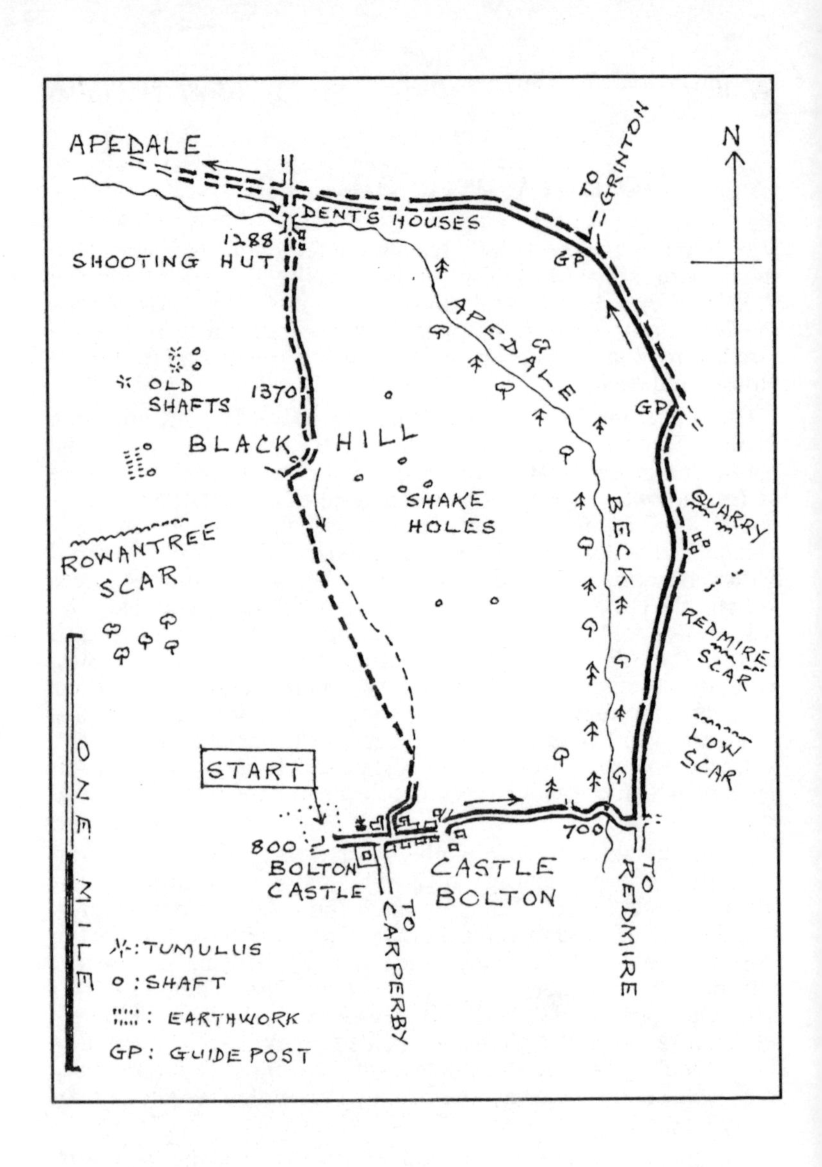

APEDALE
DENT'S HOUSES
1288
SHOOTING HUT
TO GRINTON
N
GP
APEDALE
OLD SHAFTS
1370
BLACK HILL
GP
SHAKE HOLES
BECK
QUARRY
ROWANTREE SCAR
REDMIRE SCAR
LOW SCAR
ONE MILE
START
800
700
BOLTON CASTLE
CASTLE BOLTON
TO CARPERBY
TO REDMIRE
:TUMULUS
o :SHAFT
: EARTHWORK
GP: GUIDE POST

Swaledale; take it as far as you wish to go, before returning to cross tracks near the shooting hut.

Circuit walkers now pass through a gate and over Apedale Beck on a bridge. This is National Park border country; from now on we are in the Park, having earlier been outside it. Pass the shooting hut, marked 'out of bounds', walking on a good green track by the side of a wire fence. Over to the left the chimney on Preston Moor can be seen again. On Black Hill go through a stile by the side of a gate across the road, where a whole new outlook emerges. Across Wensleydale, Penhill is prominent; the valley of Walden is to the right of it; Bishopdale goes away towards Wharfedale; and still further to the right is the distinctive shape of Addlebrough, seen over the stepped hills above Carperby — Wegber Scar and Great Wegber, rising to Woodhall Greets.

Descending, the scar seen on the immediate right is Rowantree Scar. A clear track leads to an enclosed farm lane — muddy in wet weather — and comes into the village 150 yards from the castle. In the wall at the junction a tap is conveniently placed for the benefit of the thirsty traveller.

Bolton Castle

Aysgarth Falls

THE HUB of all Wensleydale is its most popular beauty spot — Aysgarth Falls. Adequately signposted and properly provided with car park, toilets, information centre and café, it may however be thought hardly necessary to give it a chapter in this book. Some people see only the upper falls and come away thinking they have seen all there is to offer, missing the grandest of them all — the lower falls. The following information is taken from the *Yorkshire Dales National Park Guide* issued for the Countryside Commission; 'The three sets of falls at Aysgarth are caused by the outcropping of hard bands in the Yoredale Series and attract many visitors. The drop allowed the construction of mills and the mill by the bridge (which itself dates from 1539) is famous because it supplied the red flannel for the shirts for Garibaldi's army.'

Use the car park, which is on the Carperby side of the river. Walk down the road to two notices on the left directing you to 'Middle Force and Lower Force' and 'Keep to top footpath.' Follow this for 100 yards and turn right for a sight of the middle force by scrambling down the hillside on polished tree roots. This fall, which is quite impressive, is often missed, especially in the summertime when the leaves are thick on the trees. Regain the footpath and pass through a small iron swing gate, following the worn path as far as a stile in the fence on the right, signposted to 'Lower Force.' From the stile go straight down to a viewpoint of the falls, from which you may first prefer to walk upstream to the top of the falls before returning through the woods to a cleft leading down to the rock floor at the water's edge. Here the clean rocks, beside rushing water and beneath cliffs topped with trees, give the spot a holiday atmosphere.

Return to the stile, from which you can simply go back the way you came and walk along the road, first to the upper falls and then by raised track to the car. Alternatively, you can complete the full circuit by picking up the track signposted to Carperby which you would have noticed earlier. The proper way to do this is to return to the signpost and take a sharp right turn.

The track to Hollin House Farm is clearly marked by 'path' signs, yellow arrows, white posts and stiles; the way through the farm yard is also plainly indicated. Behind and across the Dale is Penhill; in front, Bolton Castle comes into sight. Follow the farm road until a 'Footpath' notice is seen painted on the wall on the right beside a tractor trail. Turn on this trail, following it 250 yards as far as a stile over the wall on the right. Do not go over it but turn squarely left to

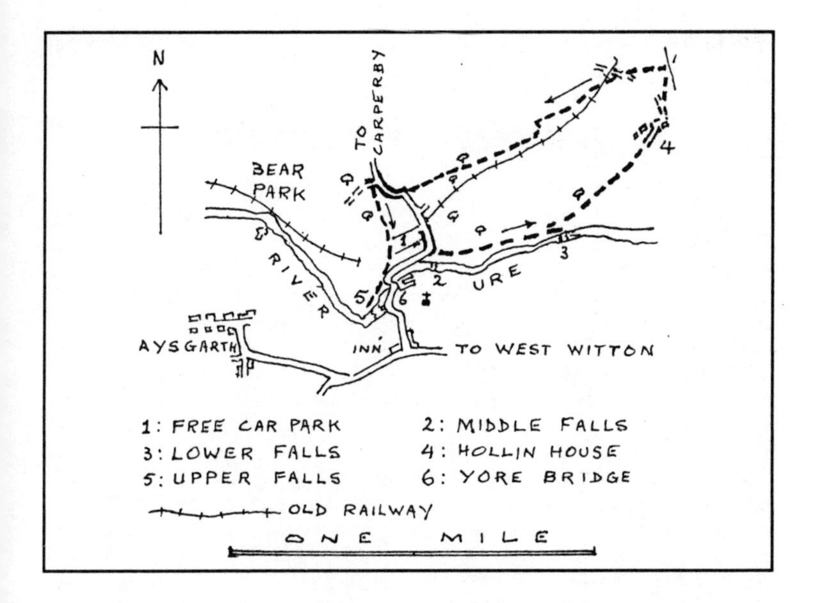

walk over grazing ground — marshy in parts — to a signpost by the side of the farm road. Follow the direction of the arm indicating Aysgarth, over a stile, to cut across the corner of a field to another stile. Cross the disused line and turn left, walking on the right-of-way which is just outside the old railway boundary.

Pass through a stile in the wall ahead and keep beside a wire fence on the left, a field away from the railway tracks. At the end of the field go through a gate on the left and walk towards the line, but turn right just before it, going through three fields to a gate into a wood. Twenty yards later turn right on a single track, then left, to continue in the line of march, going slightly uphill through trees and out on to the Carperby road by a stile at the side of a gate.

On the road turn right and, after a hundred yards, left through gates into Bear Park. Turn left immediately, passing to the right of a Knoll and then bearing left to go through a gate in a wire fence. Continue downhill across a field to a stile in another wire fence, which leads to a path and an iron gate. Cross the old railway and turn left down steps to the car park — but the Upper Force is still to be visited. Take a Nature Trail track down to Yore Bridge and enter the grounds of Bear Park again by a wooden gate. Here it is pleasant to take in the beauty of the upper falls splashing over mossy rocks — not so dramatic as those already observed but the favourite of those who prefer the gentler scene. The view from the bridge is delightful but look out for traffic. Return to the car park by the footpath.

Askrigg's Waterfalls

Note: Changes in the Mill Gill/Whitfield Gill footpath network are likely in the near future. These will be waymarked.

TO ADD to the simple enjoyment of beauty, some reference to the geology of Wensleydale, responsible for the creation of much of its splendour, is appropriate. Arthur Raistrick's chapter on 'Geology and Scenery' in the *Yorkshire Dales National Park Guide* gives some helpful information. Writing about the Yoredale Series of limestone he says: 'The Yoredales are a series of thinner limestone occurring in rhythmic sequence with shale and sandstone, so that a "unit" of limestone, shale, sandstone, is repeated many times. The differing resistance to weathering of the limestone and shale is the cause of the terraces of the sides of Wensleydale and of the abundance of lovely waterfalls in all its stream-courses. The principal limestones, from the bottom upward, are Hardraw Scar, Simonstone, Middle and Main; these four are responsible for most of the obvious scars in Wensleydale. The repeated rhythmic units vary considerably in thickness and so give great variety to the scars . . . A section of the lower portion of the Yoredale Series is admirably displayed near Askrigg and in following this section one will see some fine waterfalls.'

Askrigg is the home of the authors, Marie Hartley and Joan Ingilby, whose book *Yorkshire Village* describes it in great detail. Park the car on the cobbles outside the stately parish church of St Oswald and follow the road to the right of it, marked 'No through road. Footpath to Mill Gill Force.' Leaving the houses on this narrow way, a gate across the road will soon be reached on which is a notice saying 'Private road.' On the right is a signpost 'Millgill Force' pointing to a trod across the field which leads to the north end of the charming complex of mill and farm buildings. Take this route and join a footpath beside the stream which is here known as Mill Gill Beck. Below, it is called Paddock Beck; in its higher reaches it has the name Whitfield Gill Beck.

Continue by the side of the stream as far as a finger post which points the way to Mill Gill Force across a substantial footbridge. Turn right after passing through a stile, keeping to the wall on the right and going through a series of stiles — in single file please. Soon you should hear the sound of a distant waterfall and if the trees are not in full leaf you should also see it; a stile in the wall on the right leads to another beside a finger post indicating Mill Gill Force. A good stony path leads down to the fall, and as you round a bend you will be impressed by its height — similar to that of Hardraw, from which the limestone takes it name, except that this is a broken fall. A fine pool is near the foot, and in the vegetation there are plenty of specimens for the botanist.

Return to the finger post and turn right at the other side of the wall, following a green cart-way up the hill. Across the dale on the left is Bainbridge, with the Roman fort to the left of it: behind the fort is Addlebrough; and rising steadily towards Wether Fell to the right of the village is the Roman road. Turn through a stile on the right, immediately past a farm building with a corrugated iron roof. Make for the farm straight ahead, turning right on reaching it and going through an iron gate towards power cable posts. Walk down to and across the bridge below Leas House. Bear to the left of Leas House, sloping upwards to join a bridleway which leads to a gate and the farm drive, continuing to the junction with the enclosed road along Askew Top.

To extend the walk half a mile each way, turn left up the road. At the end of it is a gate, just beyond which is a 'V' stile in the wall on the left to a path which gives views of the impressive Whitfield Gill Force. But there is no right of way beyond the gate. Return to Leas House drive end and continue down the lane along the basic route.

All walkers will certainly enjoy the straightforward walking down this lane, giving an opportunity to take in details of the Wensleydale

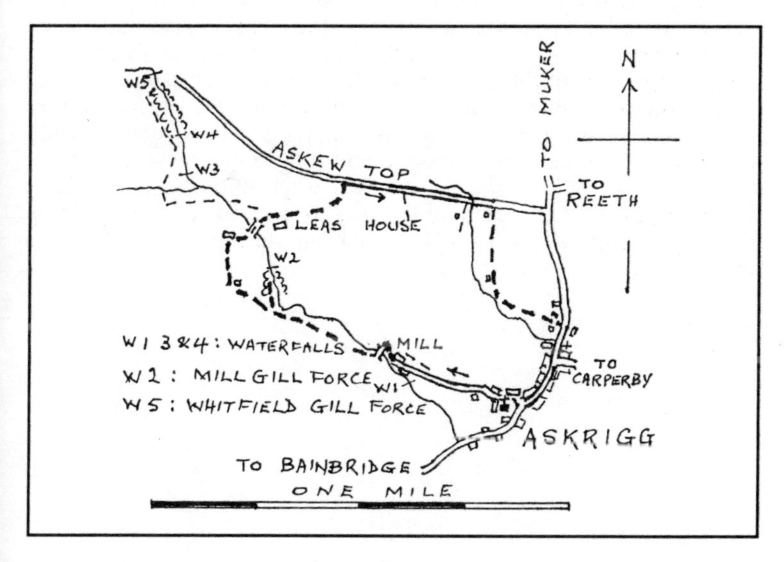

The Mill, Askrigg

scene ahead, with Penhill in the background. To the left front are the 'steps' of the hills seen from the other side in Walk 9, an interesting exercise being to identify the Yoredale Series. Cross a water splash, either through the water or over a footbridge. About 120 yards beyond is a large ash tree on the right. Go through a stile immediately past it and walk in the field on the left of a wall and a barn 50 yards from the tree. With the church tower in sight ahead, pass to the right of an attractive dry valley and leave the field where it narrows to the neck and a gate opening. The stream already crossed in the lane will be seen ahead but do not cross it again — bear left and walk beside it on a cart track to a stile and a gate, keeping near to the stream all the way to the village. Turn right on the tarmac road so as to explore Askrigg on the way back to the church.

Wether Fell and Bardale

SOME fine walking country lies to the south of the river Ure between Bishopdale and Widdale. Semer Water is in the middle of the region, overlooked by Addlebrough, of distinctive shape.

Take the car to Bainbridge, well kept round a village green and famous for its hornblower and its Roman fort on Brough Hill — a drumlin. Motor to Marsett (3½ miles) via Countersett and Semer Water, leaving the car on the grass by the stream in the village. Return to the first lane immediately on the left, where there should be a public footpath sign although this was damaged when last visited.

Follow the gated farm road, turning left at the end through the gate leading to the farm 'Bella or Knight Close'. But instead of going down to the farm, keep to the wall on your right and go through a wicket gate in it. Go uphill half left to a stile about mid way in the cross wall. Go over it and continue in the same direction to a stile in another crossing wall. Keeping in the line of march, the crossing of the stream on the left is at the top end of a steep-sided cutting, soon after which will be seen a stile in the next wall. On the other side cross the field to a gap in the wall ahead and then diagonally to a stile near the corner of the field, which is a few yards to the right of a gap in the adjoining wall on the left. Over the stile, bear left uphill to pick up a double track bearing half left.

The Roman road, between walls, is now in sight. Join it at a metal gate and turn left. This is a good stony, grassy road, ideal for walkers. Looking back the track is typically Roman — long and straight — but ahead it curves upwards round Wether Fell. The scene behind and to the left embraces Semer Water, Addlebrough beyond it, Penhill further away, and in good weather conditions the North York Moors on the other side of the Vale of Mowbray. Buckden Pike comes into sight on the left and as you reach the brow of the hill Pen-y-ghent is in front, slightly to the left of your line of march. The triangulation pillar, 2,015 feet, on Drumaldrace — the south-west tip of Wether Fell — is obscured on the immediate right by the curve of the hillside.

Join the hard road linking the heads of Wensleydale and Wharfedale, and turn left at the junction with the Cam End road (now tarred but not yet shown as such on the O.S. maps). At the first gate on the left, 200 yards further on, go through it to join a double green track downhill. Rounding two bends the path will be seen to go to a

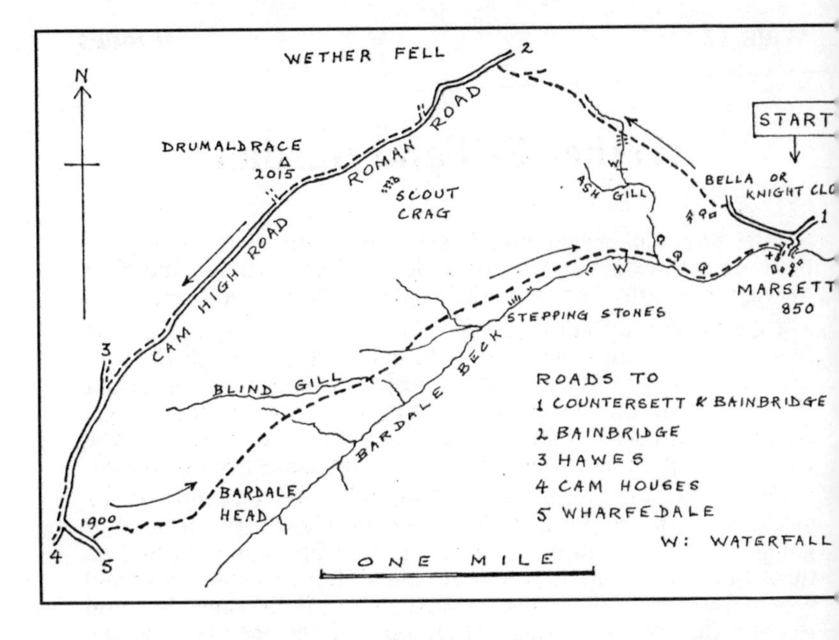

gate in a wall; do not go through the gate — instead, turn left where a single path follows the wall down Bardale.

The rest of the route is simple. Keep to the wall on your right until you have passed a group of trees, but go through a gate in the wall before reaching a stone erection in the shape of the end of a Nissen hut — which was once almost certainly its function. On the other side of the wall make straight for Semer Water, which is almost always in view on this return journey. You are now on a green track on the brow of a small spur, passing through a series of gates and over streams, the second of which is Blind Gill, suitably named because it disappears into the ground below the crossing place.

The track brings you to stepping stones over Bardale Beck, but resist the temptation to go over to the other side where there is a well-defined route down the valley (a snare leading to boggy ground). Stay on this side — which has the added merit of carrying the right of way — and enjoy the delight of walking alongside the lovely Bardale Beck. Soon you will reach a waterfall and pool. Where better, and at what better time of day, to take a plunge? Below the pool and fall the stream bed is of solid limestone, falling into an impressive little gorge containing a succession of small waterfalls. The right of way is still on the lelft bank, but the right bank gives better local views and leads to a footpath to the village of Marsett and the car.

Walk 13 **9 miles**

Semer Water and the Stake Pass

THE attractions of this walk include one of Yorkshire's few lakes, about which Marie Hartley and Joan Ingilby say: "Semer Water has many charms and a traditional story. The legend of a city sunk beneath its waters has proably a basis in fact. Here were Iron Age lake dwellings, some of which may well have been submerged by a sudden flood. A causeway leads out into the lake from the strange rocks near the enormous limestone boulder of glacial origin called the Carlow Stone, and a Bronze Age spearhead was found some years ago on the north shore."

Just outside Bainbridge, on the main road to Aysgarth, take the road to Stalling Busk — an uphill climb for 300 yards to a bend, beyond which park on the grass verge near a gate with a stile and a footpath finger post on the right. Follow the path uphill, roughly parallel to the valley of the Bain, England's shortest river, and pass to the left of an intake and building. Look back for a good view of the Roman camp on the top of the large drumlin outside Bainbridge. A single cattle trail skirts the hill ahead but keep up above it and climb over the top to a signpost in a crossing wall. Here are two stiles. Take the right-hand one and go forward over Bracken Hill. On the other side of the river is Bainbridge High Pasture, over which the Roman road takes its straight course to pass between Yorburgh, 1,686 feet, and Crag, 1,614 feet. Crag is the height rising above Semer Water which now comes into sight.

Go forward to a stile in a wall, another beside a tree and a gate in the wall beyond. Proceed downhill to a gate and stile quite close to a bend in the Bain. Keep in line of march, now with a wall and a barn on the left to pass through a gap in the next wall to a gate in the wall on the left. Turn right to continue forward, passing to the left of a barn to a gap and clear track on the left of a wall. Go through a gate at the right-hand corner of a field, now near the river again, and through a gap to a stile beside Semer Water Bridge. Turn left on the road, pass the Carlow Stone near the lake side and keep on the road when it goes uphill, looking out for the sharp edge of Addlebrough ahead. Cross Little Ings Bridge, pass temporary buildings on the right and, opposite Low Blean Farm, go through the gate on the right at a footpath sign.

Now, with a wall between you and the lake, go through a succession of three stiles and on to a clear track above the water, well sign-posted, which rises and forks a quarter of a mile beyond the head of

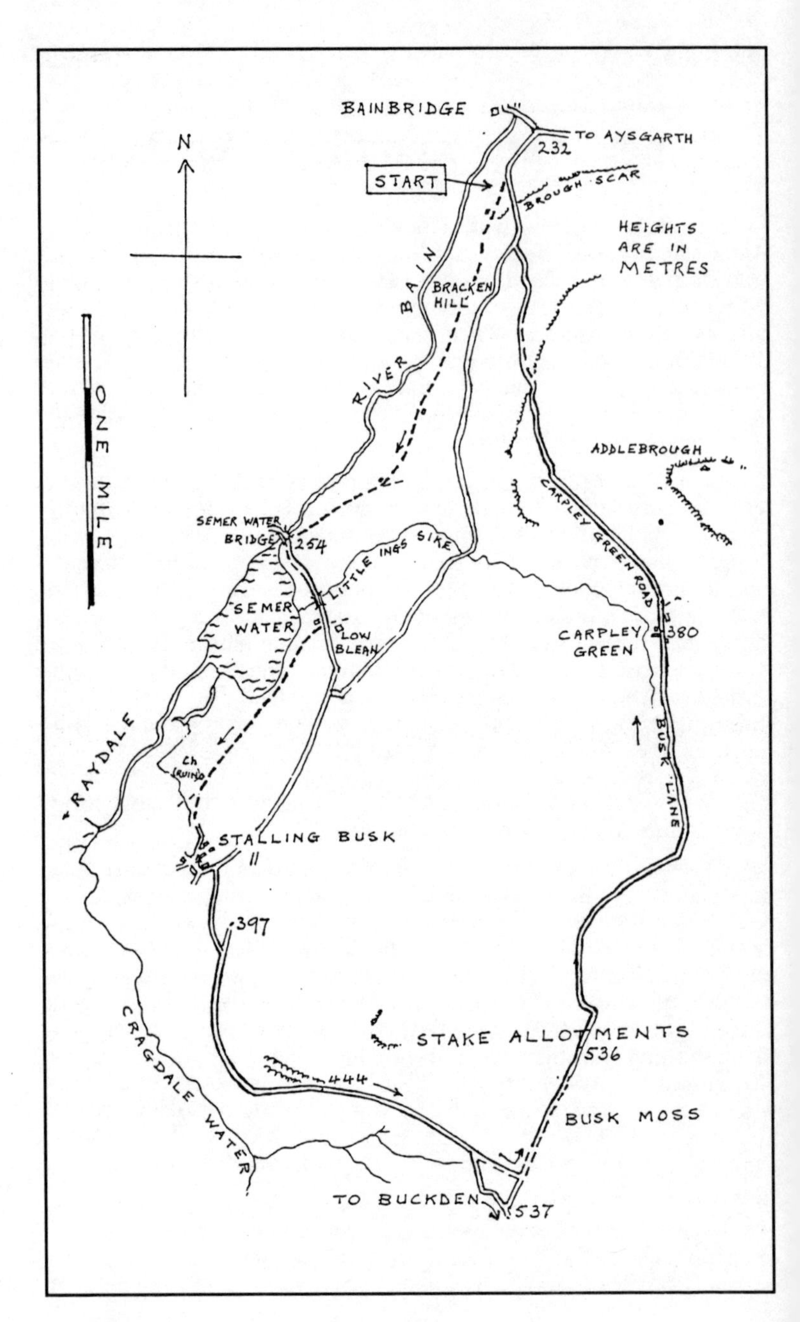
BAINBRIDGE
TO AYSGARTH
232
START
BROUGH SCAR
HEIGHTS ARE IN METRES
N
ONE MILE
RIVER BAIN
BRACKEN HILL
ADDLEBROUGH
CARPLEY GREEN ROAD
SEMER WATER BRIDGE
254
LITTLE INGS SIKE
SEMER WATER
LOW BLEAH
CARPLEY GREEN
380
BUSK LANE
RAYDALE
Ch (RUIN)
STALLING BUSK
397
CRAGDALE WATER
STAKE ALLOTMENTS
536
444
BUSK MOSS
TO BUCKDEN
537

the lake. Keep left on the clearer path, through a stile and walk uphill on the left of a wall, on the other side of which is a ruined ivy-covered church. Go uphill, with a wall on the left and a stream on the right, entering a green lane and the village of Stalling Busk. Pause to look across Raydale to the village of Marsett at the foot of Bardale, with Wether Fell behind (Walk 12).

In Stalling Busk, pass the church, phone box and posting box to arrive at a T-road. Here a decision must be made. We have now travelled a third of the distance of the full walk and there is an ascent to be made of about 700 feet. Should a return be made by going straight along the road on the left (and up the hill initially) back to the car, or by retracing steps?

Those doing the whole walk do turn left, but half-way up the hill take the turning on the right up a rough stony lane, soon to join the Stake Pass road with its better stony surface. Down on the right is Cragdale — the third of the three valleys at the head of the dale — and now there is to be a steady climb for 1½ miles on this famous Roman link between Bainbridge and Buckden in Wharfedale, fit for Land-Rovers but not for cars. Nearing the top, the road takes a sharp turn to the right, from which another acute turn (to the left) will be seen higher up. At the right-hand turn leave the road, go left through a gap in the wall, and keep straight on uphill on sheep tracks, with a wall on your left. Turn left at the first gate, joining a green track — between old walls — coming from the road.

Follow the green track over the open moor — Busk Moss — to pass through Stake Allotments. The track goes through a gate and now there is a good wall on the left and an old one on the right. Soon the route is downhill and Addlebrough is seen ahead and below, until, after a change of direction, it appears for a short time on the left. When it is again to your right front you will see a wall going away from you to the top of the hill. There is no right-of-way over it but this wall is sometimes used as a guide to the top from a track leading from the north of Carpley Green. Today our route is straight on through the farm of Carpley Green, after which the surface of the road is tarred. Semer Water comes into sight again on the left and the head of Wensleydale to the left front. Join the road from Stalling Busk; the car will soon be seen ahead.

Walk 14 **9 miles**

Hardraw and Great Shunner Fell

NO VISIT to Wensleydale would be complete without going to see England's highest waterfall above ground — Hardraw Force, a single drop of the waters of Fossdale Gill and Hearne Beck which join a mile up-stream. The waterfall is in an impressive gorge, noted for its acoustics, for here is the site of an old bandstand where brass band contests were held. To gain access, the public must pass through the bar of the *Green Dragon Inn* in the village where a small charge is made. A trip to the fall, if included in today's journey, would add a mile.

Leave the car at the west end of the village (spelt 'Hardrow' on O.S. maps, but rarely elsewhere, and surely never pronounced that way) just beyond the last building on the right which is a school. Here is a 'Pennine Way' signpost pointing to a narrow, enclosed roadway. Take this route as far as the gate leading to the open fell. Fifty yards from the gate the metalled Pennine Way bears to the left, but leave it and take the clear grassy track seen ahead. Looking back, the top of Ingleborough should soon be seen peeping over Snaizeholme Fell. The track is now the Hearne Coal Road — no longer used by miners — sometimes wide, sometimes a single path, depending on the terrain. It goes first towards a hump with a shooting house clearly seen, and then up the left-hand valley, keeping Hearne Beck down on the right. Encountering some boggy ground, the path peters out. It is as well to leave the right-of-way here to try to keep dry feet, and make towards what appears to be an overgrown spoil heap uphill on the left. Continue north-west over peat hags until the unmistakable Pennine Way is reached, liberally marked with cairns — useful guides through boggy ground. Turn right and make your way to the top of Shunner; on a fine day the summit cairn will have long been in sight.

The view from the top in good conditions is all-embracing. The Lake District mountains will already have been observed on the left on approaching the summit, as well as Wild Boar Fell and, behind it, the Howgill Fells. Looking back, the Three Peaks of Ingleborough, Whernside and Pen-y-ghent now show their full glory. Ahead, the fells at the head of Swaledale come into sight, such as Nine Standards Rigg behind Birkdale Tarn, High Seat and Hugh Seat a little nearer. For one of the best views down Swaledale itself, one must extend the walk further north on the Pennine Way to a slender beacon, adding half a mile each way.

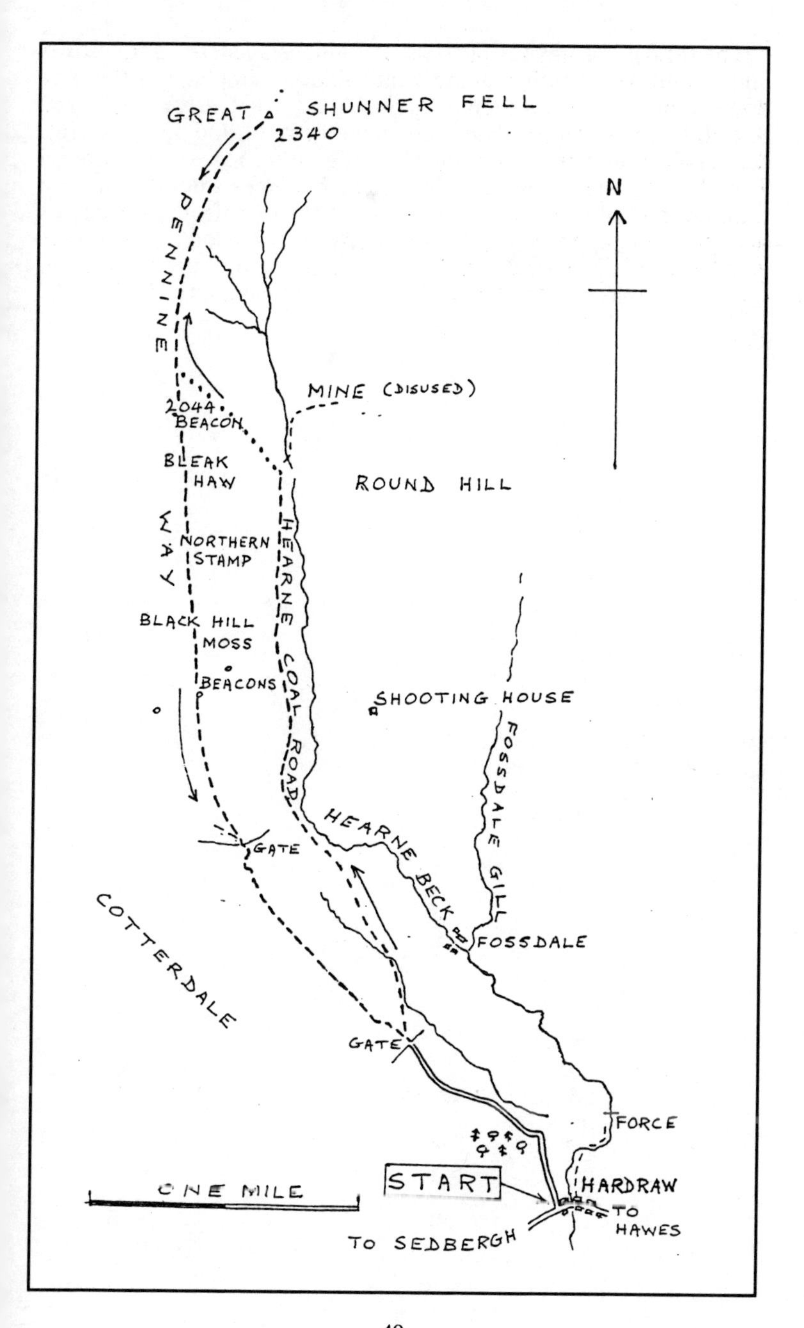
GREAT SHUNNER FELL
2340
N
PENNINE WAY
MINE (DISUSED)
2044
BEACON
BLEAK HAW
ROUND HILL
NORTHERN STAMP
HEARNE COAL ROAD
BLACK HILL MOSS
BEACONS
SHOOTING HOUSE
FOSSDALE GILL
HEARNE BECK
GATE
COTTERDALE
FOSSDALE
GATE
FORCE
START
HARDRAW
ONE MILE
TO HAWES
TO SEDBERGH

The return journey keeps to the Pennine Way all the time, cairns and a well-worn path making route finding simple. On the way down, a new feature is seen on arrival at a cairn nearly as big as the one at the top — Cotterdale is down on the right, looking peaceful. Many will regret the appearance of row upon row of conifers on Tarn Hill on the other side. The going becomes smoother as one joins another old coal road, coming in on the right from disused pits in Cotterdale, approaching the first of two gates below; between the gates, the sheep-cropped track is a delight. At the second gate the outward path is joined, steps beng retraced through the lane.

Walk 15 **3 miles**

Hell Gill

HELL GILL, a dramatic gorge separating North Yorkshire and Cumbria, marks the north-western boundary of Wensleydale. Hell Gill Beck turns north, becoming the river Eden which empties into the Solway: less than half a mile away is the river Ure, going south and east to the Humber. In fact, splashes of rain on Ure Head, a mile upstream, can fall inches from each other and take oppsite directions on their way to the sea.

From the *Moorcock Inn,* which is on the Hawes/Sedbergh road, take the road towards Kirkby Stephen for two miles, leaving the car at Shaw Paddock before the road takes a sharp left turn under the railway — the grass verge is wide enough. Walk straight forward at the bend, passing through a gateway by the side of some sheep pens on a good stone farm road. On rounding the corner, the first of the fells of Mallerstang Common — the beautiful valley of the upper Eden — comes into sight. This is Wild Boar Fell, a steepsided double 'table mountain.' Over the first bridge across the river Ure, leave the farm road and go straight forward on a green track to pass over the Ure for the last time on a small earth and stone bridge. After bearing to the right uphill, the track goes over well drained limestone land with scars in evidence on both sides. The trees ahead are at Hell Gill bridge; the farm below the bridge bears the same name. The track joined just before the bridge is the High Way, an ancient trail from Hawes to Mallerstang, via Cotter End, now used in part by the Y.H.A. for the annual 'Mallerstang Marathon,' a 25 mile walk from the old Garsdale Head Youth Hostel embracing High Seat, Nine Standards Rigg, Tailbridge Hill, Wild Boar Fell and Turner Hill.

Looking over the parapet at the bridge, you will be surprised to see the depth of Hell Gill, with the water — almost hidden by vegetation — swirling down below. There is no right of way upstream, and protection from the dangerous gorge is provided by a wall on the right bank and a wire fence on the left, but it is worth encircling these obstacles for a view of the stream tumbling into the gill. Here among the bare, rippled, limestone slabs above a plunging pool, one could establish a picnic place, from which one could wander upstream at will, observing the beck bickering and tumbling, gaining growth and strength, and acquiring character which deserves more notability than it possesses in this remote part of the Pennines.

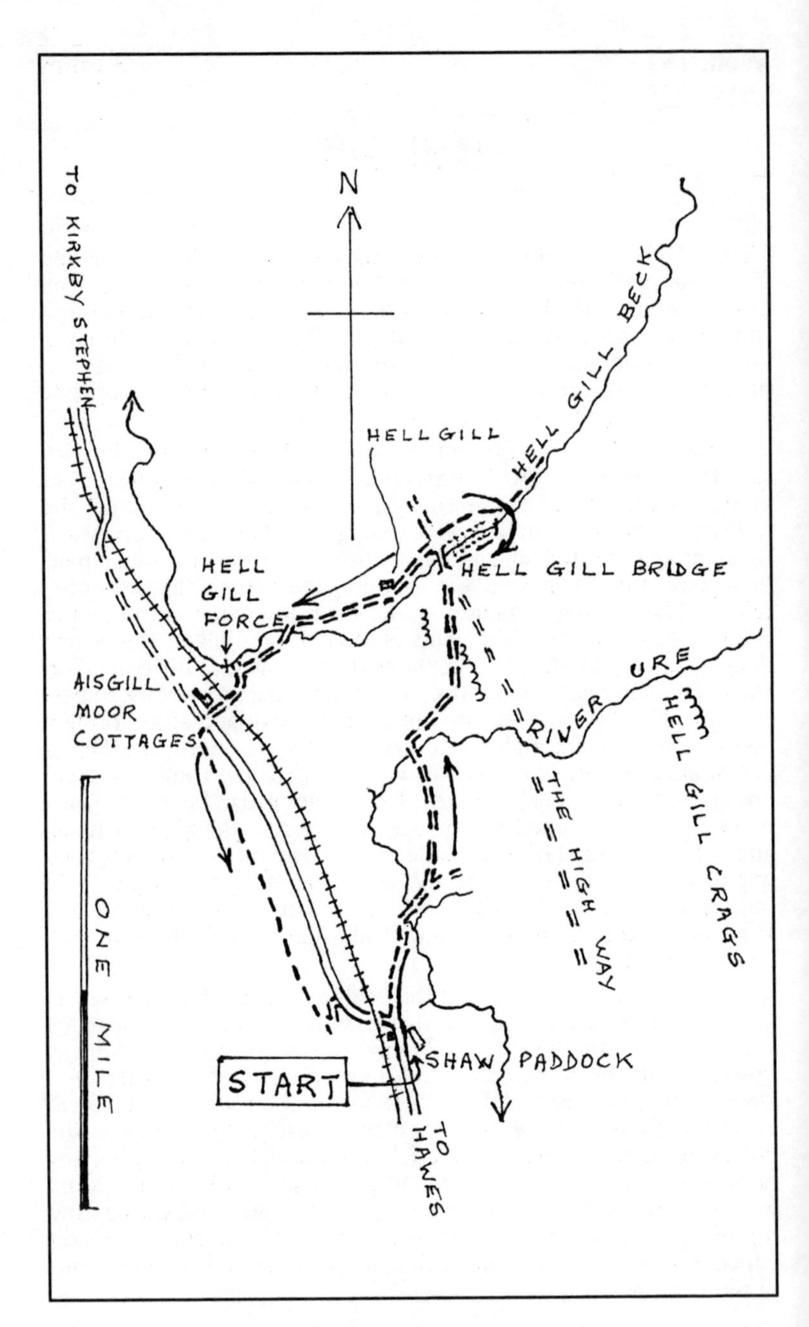
N
TO KIRKBY STEPHEN
HELL GILL BECK
HELLGILL
HELL GILL BRIDGE
HELL GILL FORCE
AISGILL MOOR COTTAGES
RIVER URE
HELL GILL CRAGS
THE HIGH WAY
ONE MILE
START
SHAW PADDOCK
TO HAWES

Return to the bridge, cross it again (assuming the Gill has been encompassed in a clockwise direction) and go thrugh the gate immediately on the left. Pass the farm of Hell Gill, continuing on the farm road — with occasional diversions for more views of the Gill — and cross a wooden bridge. At a sharp left-hand bend, you should hear the sound of water falling. If you are not yet satisfied with so much beauty, go over to the fall, Hellgill force, 50 yards from the road, where you will find another Hardraw — not so high, but carrying more water, and a fine sight.

Soon you will come to a bridge over the railway. Pause and look back for a view of the fells of Mallerstang Edge — High Seat, three miles away; Hangingstone Scar, unmistakable and a little nearer; and Hugh Seat, behind it and along the line of an old wall forming the boundary of both the county and the National Park. The main road is reached at Aisgill Moor Cottages, where tea and coffee are advertised and a seat is provided opposite. Turning left, a three quarter mile walk along the road would bring you back to Shaw Paddock.

You could, however, avoid road walking by crossing to the other side, passing through a gateway and turning left. Keep to the right of a fence and then a wall, go through a gate in a cross wall and continue forward, keeping a wall on your left. Make for a gate in the wall ahead and beyond it, walk on a grassy track through reeds. At the brow of the hill look to the railway line on the left and see a bridge over the road — we shall eventually pass under it. Still keeping a field away from the road, on approaching the bridge observe a gate in the wall on the left. Leaving the right of way, go through the gate and down to the road through another gate. Some 200 yards of road walking brings you to the bridge. The car is round the bend on the other side of the railway line.

Bibliography

GENERAL

Hartley, M., and Ingilby, J., *The Yorksire Dales* (Dent, 1963).

Hartley, M., and Ingilby, J., *Life and Tradition in the Yorkshire Dales* (Dent, 1968).

Raistrick, A., *Old Yorkshire Dales* (David & Charles, 1968).

Raistrick, A., *The Pennine Dales* (Eyre & Spottiswoode, 1968).

Simmons, I. G. (edit.), *Yorkshire Dales National Park* (H.M.S.O.).

Wightman, P., *Yorkshire Dales* (Yorkshire Dales Tourist Association, 1968).

The Yorkshire Dales (Ward, Lock, 7th edit., 1968).

AGRICUTURE AND INDUSTRY

Calvert, T. C., *The Story of Wensleydale Cheese* (Dalesman, 1946).

Clough, R. T., *The Lead Smelting Mills of the Yorkshire Dales* (Author, 1960).

Raistrick, A., *Pennine Walls* (Dalesman, 1946, and subsequent editions).

Raistrick, A., and Jennings, B., *A History of Lead Mining in the Pennines* (Longmans, 1965).

ARCHAEOLOGY AND HISTORY

Hartley, M., and Ingilby, J., *Yorkshire Village* (Dent, 1953).

Raistrick, A., *Prehistoric Yorkshire* (Dalesman, 1964).

Raistrick, A., *The Romans in Yorkshire* (Dalesman, 1960).

GEOGRAPHY AND TRAVEL

Brown, A. J., *Fair North Riding* (Country Life, 1952).

King, C. A. M., *The Yorkshire Dales: a description of the Ordnance Survey one-inch sheet 90, Wensleydale (Geographical Association, 1960).*

NATURAL HISTORY AND GEOLOGY

Raistrick, A., and Illingworth, J., *The Face of North-West Yorkshire* (Dalesman, 1967).

Raistrick, A., *The Ice Age in Yorkshire* (Dalesman, 1968).

PLACE NAMES

Smith, A. H., *The Place Names of the North Riding of Yorkshire* (Cambridge University Press, 1928).

BUILDINGS

Pevsner, N., *Yorkshire: the North Riding (Buildings of England)* (Penguin, 1968).

Waddington, F., *The Abbeys and Castles of Yorkshire* (Author, 1908).

Walton, J., *Homesteads of the Yorkshire Dales* (Dalesman, 1947).

Long Distance Walks passing through the region

THE PENNINE WAY

Binns, A. P., *Walking the Pennine Way* (Gerrard, 1966).

Marriott, M., *Shell Book of the Pennine Way* (Queen Anne Prerss, 1966).

Oldham, K., *The Pennine Way,* (Dalesman, 1960).

Stephenson, T., *The Pennine Way* (H.M.S.O., 1969).

Wainwright, A., *Pennine Way Companion* (Westmorland Gazette, 1968).

MALLERSTANG MARATHON

An annual event organised by the Youth Hostels' Association, usually on the last Saturday in June. For details and entry form send stamped addressed envelope to Mr. M. Bolison, 6 Westbourne Avenue, Garforth, West Yorkshire.

THE FELLSMAN HIKE

A competitive annual event of more than 50 miles from Grassington to Ingleton, passing over Great Whernside, Buckden Pike, Middle Tongue, Fleet Moss, Dodd Fell, Snaizeholme Fell, Great Knoutberry, Blea Moor, Great Coum, Gragareth, Whernside and Ingleborough. It usually occurs on the second or third Saturday in May. For details send 9″×4″ stamped addressed envelope to: Fellsman Hike, P.O. Box 30, Keighley, West Yorkshire.